D0931505

Mestizo Nations

To Jonathan,
in friendship,

Juan E. De Castro
6/23/2004

Mestizo Nations

CULTURE, RACE, AND CONFORMITY
IN LATIN AMERICAN LITERATURE

Juan E. De Castro

The University of Arizona Press   Tucson

The University of Arizona Press
© 2002 Arizona Board of Regents
⊛ This book is printed on acid-free, archival-quality paper.
Manufactured in the United States of America
First Printing

07   06   05   04   03   02   6   5   4   3   2   1

Library of Congress Cataloging-in-Publication Data

Castro, Juan E. De, 1959–
    Mestizo nations : culture, race, and conformity in Latin American
Literature / Juan E. De Castro.
        p. cm.
Includes bibliographical references and index.
    ISBN 0-8165-2192-1 (cloth : alk. paper)
    1. Latin American literature—20th century—History and criticism.
2. Mestizaje in literature. 3. National characteristics, Latin American,
in literature. 4. Nationalism in literature. 5. Literature and
society—Latin America. I. Title.
    PQ7081 .C348 2002
    860.9′355—dc21   2001008064

British Library Cataloguing-in-Publication Data
A catalogue record for this book is available from the British Library.

Este libro está dedicado a la memoria de
Delia Lava de Céspedes, mi nona.

contents

acknowledgments

Parts of chapter 4, "José de Alencar's *Iracema:* Mestizaje and the Fictional Foundation of Brazil," appeared originally as "José de Alencar's *Iracema:* The Ambiguities of Writing as Translation" in *Mester* 24, no. 1 (1995). Chapter 8, "Richard Rodriguez in 'Borderland': The Relocation of the Discourse of Mestizaje," is an edited and revised version of "Richard Rodriguez in Borderland: The Ambiguity of Hybridity," published in *Aztlán: A Journal of Chicano Studies* 26, no. 1 (2001).

I must first express my gratitude to Lucille Kerr. She not only read and commented on the very early drafts of what was to become this book, but has also provided me with an example of what it means to be a true scholar. Roberto Ignacio Díaz assisted me with his polyglot knowledge of world literature, his unusual mastery of style in both English and Spanish, and more important, his friendship. Randal Johnson always has been generous with his extensive knowledge of all things Brazilian, as well as with his warm support. Anthony Kemp's enthusiasm for this project has played a major part in motivating the rewrites and additions that culminated in this book; not the least of his contributions is suggesting its title.

Half of the essays that constitute this book have been written within the last two years. This would have been impossible without the generous support of my colleagues at the Division of Liberal Arts and International Studies at the Colorado School of Mines, among whom I have to single out Arthur Sacks, director of the division, and Carl Mitcham, who gladly lent me his philosopher's eye. I also need to extend my gratitude to the anonymous readers of the University of Arizona Press, as well as my editors, Kirsteen E. Anderson, Nancy Arora, and especially Patti Hartmann. Needless to say, without their enthusiasm for this book, nothing would have been possible. My brother, Paul José De Castro, helped me with his expertise on Cuban music. Despite my intellectual debt to all these people, it should be obvious that the flaws that remain are my exclusive responsibility.

On a more personal level, this book would have been impossible without the unflagging support of my wife, Magdalena. I also want to express my gratitude to my mother, Dahlia Oritz. This book, like everything worthwhile I do, is dedicated to the memory of my grandmother, Delia Lava de Céspedes.

introduction

The last couple of decades have seen the proliferation of books about nations, nationalism, and the role played by literature in their constitution and development. It is tempting to see in this rise in intellectual interest the exemplification of one of Hegel's classic dicta. Like Minerva's owl, academic interest in the nation lifts into flight at a time when this collective entity experiences a dimming of its once-blinding light. Today, local industries wither under the furious impact of globalization; Nike sneakers are the objects of desire of many a Third World child (even if the brand name is pronounced to rhyme with "like"); recordings by Madonna, Dr. Dre, or Ricky Martin substitute for the once-vital *corrido, fado,* or *tango* traditions that fade into nostalgia; the beaming faces of Julia Roberts, Brad Pitt, and Jennifer Lopez (without an accent mark) give their subtitled benedictions to audiences in Berlin, Taipei, and Bogota, at twenty-four frames per second.

This process of globalization, which I have described somewhat impressionistically, not only weakens the nation but entails its redefinition. After all, the nation, understood in its institutional form of the state, is, at least in the foreseeable future, still indispensable to the economic processes of globalization. Thus, rather than being fully discarded, national identities constituted during the nineteenth and first half of the twentieth centuries—the halcyon days of nation building—are being modified to account for this brave new world in which we live. Conceptual boundaries are not only being torn down, they are also being rebuilt, though now they may be porous, on occasion translucent.

Since we are experiencing a process in which national and postnational, intranational and supranational identities are being built, renegotiated, and reconstructed, a study of nineteenth- and twentieth-century conceptualizations of the nation possesses more than merely antiquarian interest. These early conceptualizations of the nation are still the best-known models of how collective identities can be built. Even for those opposed to the undeniably totalizing and totalitarian aspects of the nation, these early constructions of identity serve as cautionary examples or—in that frequent paradox—as that which by being resisted ends up defining its putative opposite.

The fields of Latin American studies and Latin American literature have not been exempt from this recent interest in the construction of national identity. Following in the footsteps of Benedict Anderson's foundational study, *Imagined Communities: Reflections on the Origin and Spread of Nationalism* (first published in 1983)—among the many virtues of which one must count the foregrounding of the Americas, including Latin America, as paradigmatic examples of what constitutes a nation—Latin Americanists have investigated the construction of national identity. Most of these studies develop Anderson's insight that literature plays a crucial role in the formation of the nation and nationalism, rather than being their manifestation, as the Romantics had argued.

Among the many excellent book-length analyses of the relationship between literature and the construction of national identity in Latin America and the Americas as a whole, I must single out Doris Sommer's *Foundational Fictions: The National Romances of Latin America* (1991) and Renata Wasserman's *Exotic Nations: Literature and Cultural Identity in the United States and Brazil, 1830–1930* (1994). In *Foundational Fictions,* Sommer analyzes key nineteenth-century Spanish American and Brazilian novels that, through the thematic and rhetorical fusion of romantic and national narrative, imbricate gender and national identity in the constitution of new independent (as opposed to colonial) Latin American subjects. As Sommer (1991, xi) states, "The books construct Eros and Polis upon each other." Wasserman, who in several instances refers to Sommer's groundbreaking study, turns aspects of Anderson's argument on its head. She emphasizes the role played by the reading and reinterpretation of European narratives of American exoticness in the development of Brazilian and North American national narratives. It must be noted, however, that this emphasis on the role played by European narratives does not imply a rejection of the central importance of literature in the constitution of (North and South) American identity, but rather an identification of a genealogy for hemispheric national identities.

Although both studies, as well as Anderson's and others', are exemplary readings of the problematic of nation and narration, I have taken a somewhat different course in *Mestizo Nations*. As a rule, Sommer, Wasserman, and most other critics have downplayed the role played by non-novelistic texts in this imagining of Latin American national identities. While no one can deny the importance of Latin American "foundational" and "exotic" novels in the construction of the area's national identities, it is necessary to take into account not only other literary narrative and non-narrative texts, such as short stories and poems, but also texts arising in fields such as the social sciences, journalism, and music that have played an equally significant role in the creation of nationalistic feelings and identities. In addition to analyses of literary narratives (novelistic and non-novelistic ones), *Mestizo Nations* therefore includes studies of extra-literary texts belonging to the fields of sociology, journalism, and music. Thus, it should be evident that in the book's subtitle, *Culture, Race, and Conformity in Latin American Literature,* "literature" is used in its most general meaning.

But of equal or greater interest than the variety of texts studied is the analysis of the manner in which these heterogeneous writings are inter-related. I argue that the narratives, novels, essays, and songs studied in *Mestizo Nations* are all informed by what could be called the discourse of *mestizaje*. Thus at the core of my study of Latin American constructions of national identity is the identification, description, and analysis of the discourse of mestizaje, a word which, while literally meaning "miscegenation," can be understood as proposing the creation of a homogeneous culture or race out of Amerindian, African, and European (Spanish or Portuguese) elements. This discursive tradition originated in the attempt by the Latin American colonial *criollo* (Euro-American) elites to rhetorically ground their struggle for independence from Spain and Portugal in the history of Amerindian resistance. The discourse of mestizaje proposes that it is possible and desirable to construct a nation out of heterogeneous populations.

Despite its colonial origin, the discourse of mestizaje should not be seen as belonging exclusively to the past. On the contrary, one of the central points made in this study is that despite the justified criticisms leveled against the notion of mestizaje—that it is a covert name for assimilation, even ethnocide—its basic tropes and ideas are still being recycled and frequently continue to constitute the basis on which contemporary critics and artists interpret the problems faced in contemporary Latin America and even the United States. In *Mestizo Nations,* I argue that the discourse of mestizaje can be seen as both a forerunner of and an influence on some important postmodern and multicultural versions of identity proposed during recent decades.

The texts studied in *Mestizo Nations* have been chosen because they exemplify certain aspects and problems present in, and raised by, the discourse of mestizaje. There is, however, an element of circularity in the analysis of any discursive tradition. The claim is that this tradition underlies specific texts and provides them with images, tropes, and even themes; at the same time, these very texts are used to illustrate the discourse to which they belong. Moreover, regardless of the care taken and the justifications provided, the selection of texts cannot avoid being somewhat arbitrary. It is, after all, based on the knowledge of the person making the selection, which in turn is dependent on the vagaries of individual fate. In my case, I cannot deny the influence of my national background in my selection of three Peruvian authors. But I must also note that these texts are presented as representative of a continental rather than exclusively national tradition. I have attempted to compensate for this unavoidable circularity and contingency by grounding *Mestizo Nations* on a historical analysis of Latin American societies and discourses and by choosing a variety of texts as the basis for this examination.

This study attempts to trace the development of the discourse of mestizaje from its colonial origins to some of its more recent developments as it underpins the construction of new identities and analyses of our changing cultural and social realities. The first chapter, "The Semantic Space of the Nation," presents a brief survey of Latin American theoretical interpretations of the area's heterogeneity, and contrasts these with the approach taken in this study. "Latin America and the Discourse of Mestizaje," the second chapter, provides a historical analysis of the social and cultural contexts in which the discourse of mestizaje has developed.

The following chapters, "Ricardo Palma's *Tradiciones peruanas*" and "José de Alencar's *Iracema,*" analyze the writings of two central nineteenth-century writers who provide some of the first fully developed fictionalizations of mestizaje. "Ricardo Palma's *Tradiciones peruanas*" deals with the contradictions into which the Peruvian writer's narratives fall when he attempts to ground national difference on Amerindian subjects and cultures that are simultaneously devalued, if not outright excluded, from the conceptualization of the nation being proposed. "José de Alencar's *Iracema*" studies a classic Brazilian novel that is the most fully developed fictionalization of the classic story of mestizaje—the union of the European conquistador and the indigenous woman. Moreover, the analysis of *Iracema* permits a study of the differences between the discourse of mestizaje proposed in Brazil and in Spanish America. (Given that the cognate *mestiçagem* has not generally been used in Brazil, terms such as "racial democracy" having been preferred, I have decided to maintain the Spanish word throughout this study.)

The following two chapters study texts written in the 1920s and 1930s, the period when the discourse of mestizaje became accepted throughout most of Latin America as the basis on which national and regional identity should be constructed. "Gilberto Freyre's *Casa-Grande e Senzala*" analyzes the contradictory manner in which this classic socio-anthropological study uses the idea of mestizaje to explain the cultural and social development of Brazil and, in particular, the interaction between Portuguese and Afro-Brazilian cultures and populations. "José Carlos Mariátegui" studies the writings of one of the founders of Latin American Marxism and points out how the Peruvian's writings, despite their frequent and explicit criticisms of unrealistic celebrations of mestizaje, repeat some of the most common tropes and even ideas associated with this discursive tradition.

The final three chapters analyze versions of the discourse of mestizaje proposed during the last three decades of the twentieth century and point out the continued relevance of the questions—and answers—these texts have raised and proposed for postmodern and multicultural attempts at dealing with national and international heterogeneity. "The Black Song of Los Van Van" studies the Cuban dance band Los Van Van's use of an Afrocentric version of mestizaje in the lyrics of some of their recent songs, as well as the vision of Cuban identity it implies. "Richard Rodriguez in 'Borderland' " analyzes the manner in which the well-known Mexican American critic has reinterpreted the discourse of mestizaje, in particular the notion of the cosmic race proposed by the Mexican José Vasconcelos, and used it to interpret North American realities of the 1980s and 1990s. The last chapter, "From Mestizaje to Multiculturalism," continues the study of the relationship and relevance of the discourse of mestizaje to current problematics and theoretical proposals. In particular, it identifies the points of contact between Peruvian José María Arguedas's last novel, *The Fox from Up Above and the Fox from Down Below*, and postmodern and multicultural interpretations of identity proposed by Gloria Anzaldúa and Julia Kristeva.

This study provides a brief, incomplete, but still representative selection of texts informed by the discourse of mestizaje that cuts across chronological, linguistic, and even generic boundaries. Through the study of these texts, I attempt to map the discourse of mestizaje, to find its contradictions, its lies, and its erasures of real-life cultural, racial, and social exploitation. But the discourse of mestizaje is also an early attempt at reconciling heterogeneity with commonality. Thus, the discourse of mestizaje is a response, no matter how faulty or biased, to a problem that is every day more relevant in our contemporary world, where Eurocentric versions of identity fade as contemporary migrations bring individuals of all races, cultures, and ethnicities into daily contact with each other.

Mestizo Nations

CHAPTER ONE

The Semantic Space of the Nation

Mestizaje, Hybridity, Transculturation, Borderlands

Spanish America and Brazil are frequently seen as the privileged loci of cultural, racial, ethnic, and linguistic heterogeneity and, as a consequence, of miscegenation and cultural mixture. These "human alluvia," to use José Carlos Mariátegui's phrase (1971, 273), began with the conquistadors bringing people from all continents and cultures to a Latin America already rich in indigenous populations and civilizations to create a diversity obvious to even the most superficial observer. It is not surprising then that nineteenth-century racialism, in its pseudoscientific manifestations, finds in Latin America the exemplar of its fears and prejudices.[1] When recalling his previous warnings against the "dangers of miscegenation," Robert Knox, one of the leading lights of this spurious science, claimed that "the hybrid was a degradation of humanity and was rejected by nature. In support of this latter view, I instanced Mexico, Peru, and the Central States of America, foretelling results which none attempt now to deny" (quoted in Young 1995, 15–16). A currently popular (though infinitely less nefarious) vision of Latin American heterogeneity finds the juxtapositions of modernity with so-called primitive or traditional cultures to be the defining trait of the area. This perspective has given rise to such questionable critical literary notions as those of "magical realism" or the "real marvelous"—which have, in turn, provided the intellectual basis of a whole range of literary works that run the gamut from the excellence of *One Hundred Years of Solitude* and *The Kingdom of This World* to the mediocrity of several recent formulaic bestsellers.

But closer analysis raises problems with any supposedly exclusive claim to heterogeneity. Miscegenation and cultural mixture are far from limited to Latin America. In fact, they characterize the basic historical condition of all human groups. As anthropologist Charles Stewart (1999, 41) points out, "Syncretism describes the process by which cultures constitute themselves at any given moment in time." While one can probably state that, at least until recently, these heterogeneous human alluvia may not have been as deep in Europe and the United States as in Latin America, the fact is that all these societies have to a greater or lesser degree been built on the sediment of cultural mixture and miscegenation.

What is unique about Latin America—specifically its critical and literary traditions—is that it has recognized its own heterogeneity even as it has frequently emphasized the possibility of acquiring an identifiable identity through mestizaje. In Europe minority groups (such as the Bretons in France, the Basques in Spain, or the Welsh in Great Britain) have traditionally been excluded from any reflection on national identity. Even in the United States, where in the South and the West different ethnic and racial groups have been in prolonged contact, and miscegenation and cultural borrowing have been common, self-description has invariably coded the country's identity as white. The popular notion of the melting pot—with its implicit rejection of African American, Amerindian, Asian, and Hispanic populations and cultures, and its emphasis on Anglo values—is an expression of the limits placed on North American assessments of national heterogeneity. Needless to say, both Latin American self-awareness regarding the heterogeneous constitution of its population and culture and North American conceptual erasure of its plurality are linked to concrete historical and demographic situations that need to be examined.

Despite the fact that, as we will see, this Latin American acceptance of heterogeneity has not necessarily led to egalitarian or truly plural conceptualizations of identity, it has permitted intellectuals on occasion to reverse the Eurocentric division of intellectual labor in which, in Fredric Jameson's words, "The Third World does the practice and produces the text, and the First World delivers the theory and thinks about it" (Jameson 1998, 380). Thus hybridity and transculturation, two of the terms increasingly used in anthropology and cultural studies to discuss cultural mixture, have received their fullest theorizations in the writings of Latin American authors.[2] In fact, transculturation, a word that is now used to analyze phenomena as diverse as biblical hermeneutics and Lusophone narrative, was coined by the Cuban ethnographer and sociologist Fernando Ortiz in his celebrated *Cuban Counterpoint: Tobacco and Sugar* in 1940.

Acculturation, Transculturation, and Hybridity as Concepts of Cultural Mixture

The difference between Latin American mestizaje and the North American melting pot is replicated in that between transculturation and acculturation, the anthropological term against which Ortiz coined his neologism. While the dictionary definition of acculturation indicates the possibility of cultural mixture, general usage of the word has emphasized, as Bronislaw Malinowski points out in his introduction to *Cuban Counterpoint,* a process of near-total loss of a previous culture and acquisition of an alternative one.[3] Ortiz's term "transculturation," by contrast, includes and exceeds the signification of acculturation. Thus he writes that transculturation "does not consist merely in acquiring another culture, which is what the English word acculturation really implies, but the process also necessarily involves the loss or uprooting of a previous culture, which could be described as deculturation. In addition, it carries the idea of the consequent creation of new cultural phenomena, which could be called neoculturation" (Ortiz [1940] 1995, 103).

Ortiz's concept of transculturation has been modified and applied to the study of Latin American literature by Ángel Rama in *Transculturación narrativa en América Latina* (1982), a book surprisingly ignored outside the field of Spanish American literature. The Uruguayan critic uses transculturation as a key to understand the manner in which certain twentieth-century authors—his principal example is the Peruvian José María Arguedas—manage to integrate modern literary techniques with traditional and regional cultural and aesthetic values. At its core, however, Rama's reinterpretation of the notion of transculturation implies a departure from Ortiz's formulation in two central ways. First, Rama emphasizes regional and intranational differences in the ways transculturation is experienced. For him, an already fragmented Latin America is divided into the cosmopolitan and modernized cultures of the major cities versus the traditional and regional cultures of the hinterland, both involved in a parallel but still interrelated transculturation of European and North American modernity. Moreover, he sees this division, which cuts across the national and linguistic (both Spanish and Portuguese) areas of Latin America, as one characterized by intranational conflict. According to Rama (1982, 28), the (relatively) modern urban centers promote modernization and, therefore, eradication of traditional cultures, with the exception of their fossilized and folkloric expressions. However, regional cultures and their intellectuals are capable of resisting complete deculturation or acculturation. Thus, he believes that through their artists and intellectuals, traditional cultures are able to "take hold of the contributions of modernity, use them to revise regional cultural content, and use both regional and modern elements to compose a hybrid capable of transmitting the inheritance received. It will be a renewed inheritance, but one that can still identify with its past" (Rama 1982, 29).[4]

As can be seen in this quotation, Rama's second and main departure from Ortiz's original formulation is his attribution of agency to the regional (as well as cosmopolitan urban) cultures. In Ortiz's definition, transculturation is the inevitable result of prolonged contact among individuals (or groups) belonging to different cultures. While Ortiz vehemently rejects the notion that cultural contact implies the erasure of the "weaker" culture and, therefore, celebrates the adaptive and creative capacities of the Cuban and other populations, there is no room in his formulation for individual or collective will. Rama, on the contrary, emphasizes the possibility of the renewal of cultural inheritance by the selection of the traditional elements that are to be maintained (or rediscovered) and those modern ones that are to be incorporated into the new "transculture."[5] Rama's emphasis on traditional and regional agency derives from the fact that, as the study's title indicates, his is an analysis of narrative and, therefore, narrators. Yet in *Transculturación narrativa* there is a consistent slippage between the agency of the authors or artists and that of the regional or traditional culture to which they belong.

Critics have noted that Rama's version of transculturation is indebted to the theory of dependency popular in Latin America from the late 1960s to the early 1980s.[6] Rama's vision of the relationship between international and intranational cultures reproduces the division between center and periphery characteristic of dependency theory. However, Rama's emphasis on the agency of the traditional or regional cultures—and therefore the agency of their populations—contradicts the dependency theory assertion of the determining role of the center. If dependency theory presents history as taking place only in the European and North American center, Rama's application and extension of Ortiz's concept of transculturation to literary studies acknowledges and theorizes Latin American, as well as regional, social and literary agency.[7] Rama's version of transculturation, therefore, implies a sophisticated vision of political reality in which resistance to international and globalizing capitalism is not limited, as it frequently is in dependency theory, to the utopian possibility of revolution, but rather can be found in the everyday actions of individuals and social groups. Of course, the fact that Rama avoids the obvious pitfalls of dependency theory does not imply that no objections can be raised to his interpretations of Latin American diversity.[8]

If Rama's and, to a lesser degree, Ortiz's reflections have a national or regional horizon, Néstor García Canclini's analysis implies a postnational perspective. However, while García Canclini amazingly avoids any explicit reference to the concept of transculturation (or to the works of Ortiz or Rama) in his influential *Hybrid Cultures: Strategies for Entering and Leaving Modernity* (1995), it is possible to see his reflections on cultural mixture as a postmodern development of these earlier Latin American analyses of diversity. In fact, at least one commentator has described García Canclini's work as entailing "a new aspect of transnational transculturation" (Grandis 1997, 48). After all, García Canclini's emphasis is on the breakdown of the distinctions between high and popular culture (in all meanings of the terms), modern and traditional culture, and national (or regional) and international cultures. The consequence of this (postmodern) emphasis on the fading of conceptual and social borders is that in Latin America many different paths to (post-) modernity are presented.[9] The core of García Canclini's study is his analysis of these alternative paths, ranging from the artisans of Ocumicho who incorporate images from classic French art (e.g., Delacroix's *Liberty Leading the People*) into their traditional pottery, to Jorge Luis Borges's sly manipulation of the mass media.[10] Whereas Rama celebrates the capacity for resistance to be found in Latin America's regional cultures and Ortiz the results of transculturation in Cuba, García Canclini's emphasis is on the polysemous riches of hybrid cultural products.[11]

Several of the concepts used by García Canclini seem to be an attempt to theorize anew what Ortiz and particularly Rama had already analyzed. Thus one can argue that Rama's description of a dual cosmopolitan and regional transculturation and of the internecine struggle between these subnational cultures has its parallel in García Canclini's concept of cultural reconversion, itself subdivided into hegemonic reconversion and popular reconversion. He identifies hegemonic reconversion as the neoliberal reform of the national economy, while popular reconversion is described as those "cultural crossings . . . [that] include a radical restructuring of the links between the traditional and the modern, the popular and the cultured, the local and the foreign" (García Canclini 1995, 172). Both are manners of incorporating (and being incorporated into) modernity. Popular reconversion is a reaction not only to the cultural imperatives of international culture, however, but also to the "modern" economic conditions generated by neoliberal reforms.

Another analogue to transculturation is the twin concepts of deterritorialization and reterritorialization, which García Canclini introduces in his analysis of culture in the U.S.–Mexican border region. García Canclini defines these concepts as "the loss of the 'natural' relation of culture to geographical and social territories and, at the same time, certain relative, partial territorial relocalizations of old and new symbolic production" (p. 229). Although reterritorialization parallels transculturation in that both describe attempts to reconcile identity with incorporation into international culture (and economy), it is significant that in García Canclini's texts this process is described almost as a residue of earlier preoccupations rather than as a central ongoing process of cultural agency.[12] In fact, despite his awareness of the deepening of social injustices brought about by economic globalization and neoliberal economic reforms, García Canclini generally celebrates the process of deterritorialization. In his works, globalization is more an opportunity for social and political progress than a threat to national identity: "The conflicts are not erased, as neoconservative postmodernism claims. They are placed in a different register, one that is multifocal and more tolerant, and the autonomy of each culture is rethought—sometimes—with smaller fundamentalist risks" (p. 241). However, the manner in which these progressive results are to be achieved, or how they are supposed to compensate for the parallel social and economic havoc experienced, is never explained.

García Canclini's study of Mexican border culture presents numerous points of contact with Chicano studies of the border and the borderlands.[13] Despite the fact that in Gloria Anzaldúa's reformulation, the borderlands are as much a spatialization of Chicano consciousness as a description of the Mexican and American border cultures, they are also the spatialization of hybridity. In fact, the notion of borderlands can be seen as a postmodern relocation of hybridity from Latin America to the region near the border between Mexico and the United States (especially the North American side) and, in principle, to other border areas around the world. If for critics such as Ortiz, Rama, or García Canclini, the study of hybridity is rooted in the analysis of Latin American history and culture, theorists of the borderlands find in Chicano cultural products the privileged examples of positive cultural mixture.[14] This emphasis on North American hybridity reflects the fact that the United States is today arguably the most heterogeneous nation in the world. The human alluvia, no longer principally European, now find in the United States their central destination—with Mexicans and Latin Americans constituting a large percentage of this new immigration.

The Discourse of Mestizaje

In this chapter, I have pointed toward these Latin American (and more briefly) Chicano analyses of cultural mixture in order to situate my own study of culture, race, and conformity in Latin American literatures. The central topic of *Mestizo Nations* is the discourse of mestizaje that is constituted by texts celebrating miscegenation or cultural mixture as the basis for conceiving a homogeneous national identity out of a heterogeneous population. There are numerous parallels between ostensibly scientific interpretations of heterogeneity proposed by Ortiz, Rama, and García Canclini and the discourse of mestizaje, and one could argue that the latter is the soil from which these scientific reflections spring. However, concepts such as transculturation and hybridity are not able to describe fully the texts I have chosen to study. If transculturation and hybridity attempt to analyze Latin American heterogeneity, the discourse of mestizaje uses that heterogeneity paradoxically to imagine a common past and a homogeneous future. The study of the discourse of mestizaje thus necessarily begins at a thematic level with the examination of story and tropes, although without disregarding formal elements or their cultural provenance. While an analysis emphasizing hybrid or transcultural elements in a text or work of art attempts to describe the presence of elements belonging to different cultures—as do Rama's analysis of the presence of Quechua music in Arguedas's *Deep Rivers* and García Canclini's study of European influences in the ceramics produced in Ocumicho—they generally do not account for the manner in which these texts thematically (and sometimes formally) produce a national semantic space—what one may term the "nation effect" of the discourse of mestizaje. However, given that they imagine and ultimately celebrate a national or Latin American identity, Ortiz's and Rama's texts as a whole may themselves be seen as exemplars of this discursive tradition. (Garcia Canclini's writings, moreover, can be interpreted as presenting a postmodern take on the discourse of mestizaje in which the signification of national homogeneity is consistently postponed.)

Contemporary critics, such as Antonio Cornejo Polar, have warned against the use of mestizaje as a category in literary analysis, noting that it "offers harmonic images of what is obviously disaggregated and contradictory, proposing figurations that in reality are only pertinent to those to whom it is useful to imagine our societies as smooth and non-conflictive spaces of coexistence" (Cornejo Polar 1998, 8). By contrast, I argue that it is precisely these harmonic images that must be analyzed in order for the contradictions and aporias that lie hidden beneath the smoothness of identity to be brought into focus. The importance of the analysis of the discourse of mestizaje is rooted in the need to uncover the social and cultural oppositions hidden by its veneer of homogeneity. This need is magnified not only by the fact that the discourse of mestizaje is still grounding discussions on identity in Latin America, but also that its attempt to reconcile cultural, racial, and ethnic heterogeneity with national identity constitutes an important precedent for current North American and even European discussions on multiculturalism, nationality, and postmodern plural identities.

CHAPTER TWO

Latin America and the Discourse of Mestizaje

Culture, Race, and Conformity

Although it would seem possible to separate the concepts of race and nation (the former referring principally to the sharing of genetic characteristics by a human group, the latter to the sharing of a political and geographical identification), one cannot ignore the fact that any attempt to define a nation, or to establish a national identity, inevitably becomes entangled with the question of race. The imbrication of these two concepts is evident in the attempts at national definition with which we are familiar in Europe and the Americas.

Since the interrelationship of these two words is already present in their etymologies and semantics, the connection between one concept and the other is not surprising. The source for "nation" and its cognates is the Latin verb *nasci,* literally "to be born." But already in Latin the derived noun *natio* was used for "species" or "race" (Ayto 1990, 361). The word "nation" was introduced into the English language in the late thirteenth century and maintained its Latin meaning of "racial group" (Williams 1983, 213). The etymology of "race" is, however, not as clearly understood.[1] It was not until the sixteenth century that the term, with the sense of a shared line of descent, was adopted into English from the French; by 1600 its meaning was "extended from traceable specific offspring to much wider social, cultural, and national groups" (Williams 1983, 248–49). The conceptual interrelationship between "nation" and "race" has continued until the present day.

Race as a Basis for Nationhood

Modern definitions and theories of the nation, nationality, and national-ism date back to the late nineteenth century, a period when racialist thought was hegemonic.[2] The fact that the current definitions of race and nation came into use at about the same time in the nineteenth century led to a further muddling of the already confused relationship between these concepts, because both racialism and nationalism not only connected both concepts at an intellectual level, but based their popular appeal on the emotional response to this linkage.

In its application of racist beliefs to the biological and social sciences, the racialism of the second half of the nineteenth century implied a para-digm shift in Western thought. Whether for theological reasons (such as the belief in the Adamic origin of humanity) or for biological reasons (such as the fertility of multiracial individuals), most earlier thinking had accepted the unity of humanity. Even the persecution of the Jews and Moriscos in Spain during the fifteenth, sixteenth, and seventeenth centuries—characterized by a preoccupation with "purity of blood" that can be interpreted as anticipating racialism—did not deny this theoretical equality.[3]

Clearly, this egalitarianism did not hinder or even contradict the rise of colonialism in late-Renaissance Europe. Even the radical version of egalitarianism prevalent during the Enlightenment saw the unity of hu-manity as one of potentiality rather than actuality.[4] Colonialism could thus be justified by its presumed pedagogic function of creating an en-vironment where non-Western individuals could become acquainted with Western civilization and progressively assimilate the culture of their European "tutors," who were in principle assumed to exemplify the full-est development of human potential (Young 1995, 32–34). Generalizing to the extreme, one can conclude that according to Enlightenment thought, until equality between Europeans and non-Europeans was achieved, colo-nialism could be justified.

The racialism of the nineteenth century denied this nominal equality of different human groups. Scientific racialism, basing itself on new sci-ences, such as phrenology, and on the reinterpretation of established disciplines in the natural and social sciences, gave scientific credence to the idea that behavioral differences among human groups had genetic rather than environmental origins. This pseudoscience, which became the scientific orthodoxy of the day, proclaimed a hierarchy among the different races, which were considered by some to constitute different and discrete species.[5] The logical consequence of this new mode of thinking was to define the unequal relationships between different human groups not as a temporary situation, but as a necessarily permanent and natural reflection of an intrinsic inequality among the races. In its most extreme and virulent versions, scientific racialism could lead to a complete denial of the humanity of nonwhite races, since, not surprisingly, the white race was considered by these "scientists" to be superior to all others and definitive of what it meant to be human.[6]

Nineteenth-century racialism and nationalism were not grounded exclusively in theories developed in the natural sciences, but also in the theories of language and language studies of the period, what later came to be known as philology. Already in the late eighteenth century, Johann Gottfried von Herder, although a staunch believer in the idea of the unity of the human species, had described language as the expression of a national spirit. Language, for him, was not a neutral means of communication: "It is through the language of the parents that a given mode of thinking is perpetuated" (Herder 1969, 163). Since, for Herder, language is more a national than an individual phenomenon, language and nationality do not imply merely geographical accidents or secondary facts, but a difference in the way people think and interpret reality. Simplifying to the extreme, it could be argued that in Herder's thinking language is privileged as one of the origins of what could be called national difference. Although Herder was far from being a rigid nationalist, Eurocentric, or racialist thinker, his emphasis on the importance of linguistic and national difference contributed to the privileging of the national that was developing within European thought at the end of the eighteenth and throughout the nineteenth centuries.[7]

Ideas of nation and race were also reified by the discovery that the majority of European languages belonged to the same Indo-European family. That Europe was one community was believed to be discernible not only from its common linguistic heritage, but also from a presumed national or racial heritage common to all European countries. It was reasoned that, if a single original European language had in fact existed, there also had to have been a group of people that spoke that language. That original group of people was understood to be a race. Considering the progressively hegemonic position of racialism in the nineteenth century, it not surprisingly soon became common to credit this putative Indo-European race with a central civilizing role in history as they traveled from their original homeland in central Asia to Western Europe. Such a belief in the superiority of the Indo-European stock reinforced the Eurocentric racialist hierarchization of human groups. However, it also permitted the establishment of intra-European hierarchies. The closer to its Indo-European origin a language was thought to be, the closer the people were believed to be to the original Indo-European race considered the source of all European achievements. Nineteenth-century philology thereby allowed for the establishment of racial and national hierarchies, and for the complete identification between language, race, and nation.[8] To a nation corresponded one race and one language, and it was this tripartite identity (nation-race-language) that justified national projects— that is, the move to political integration and autonomy.

The relationship between race and nation, as well as that between racialism and nationalism, rests on more than linguistic and historical factors. Race and nation serve not only to classify human groups conceptually, but also lend themselves to the reification of human difference. The exclusionary thinking behind these concepts almost always leads to the establishment of hierarchies. The idea of the nation establishes a hierarchy between the national and the foreign, the former, by definition, being superior to the latter. Hierarchy and exclusion are likewise present in the idea of race: nineteenth-century racialism only actualized what was implicit in the concept. After all, if in the classification of human groups physical characteristics are assigned a central role, it is not surprising that nonphysical characteristics are synecdochically associated with the physical and that a hierarchical order among the groups is proposed.

If this identification between race, nation, and language seemed to occur in Europe, it did not, or could not, in the Americas. Although, as has been pointed out, the North and South American nation-states were the "first real models" that inspired European nationalist thought and action, the situation in the Americas differed in significant ways from that in Europe (Anderson 1991, 46). Without exception, the New World nation-states were made up of heterogeneous racial, cultural, and even linguistic groups and, thus, the European formula for constructing nationality could not be applied to the national projects of the Americas.

In the case of the United States, a variety of national, linguistic, and ethnic groups were present at the time of independence. The U.S. population consisted of settlers of British and other European descent, together with significant numbers of blacks and Amerindians. The last two groups were in principle excluded from conceptualizations of the nation because the majority of blacks were slaves, and Amerindians were routinely expelled or exterminated as their land was taken over by the colonizers. It was within this framework that the notion of the melting pot developed. The melting pot simply meant that all citizens were expected to assimilate into the mainstream society of the United States and follow the cultural, social, economic, and political standards and behaviors characteristic of the descendants of the English colonizers (i.e., the English language, economic liberalism, etc.). As immigrants began to arrive in the United States, this form of assimilation proved very successful in creating a unified nation out of individuals of diverse European national origins. Nevertheless, hidden in the apparently neutral standards and behaviors of the melting pot was a racial and cultural hierarchy that privileged white European groups. The melting pot permitted a nation of immigrants to reproduce the European national formula: one language (English), one race (white). It is only in the twentieth century, with the refusal of Native American, African American, Hispanic, and Asian American groups to occupy subordinate positions in society, and with the increase in immigration from non-European countries, that the Eurocentric assimilationism of the melting pot has proven inadequate as a policy for incorporating immigrants (and minorities) into the national society.

The case of the Latin American countries was, at first, much more complex than that of the United States. Unlike the United States, in Latin America the colonial population comprised Amerindian, black, and racially mixed majorities, in addition to the Caucasian ruling elites, who in most cases were in fact only nominally white. In 1933, Brazilian anthropologist and sociologist Gilberto Freyre described the Brazilian colonial elites as "whites and light-skinned mulattoes" (Freyre 1956, xxix), while Peruvian intellectual Manuel González Prada (1976, 290) claimed to find people of all races in even the most aristocratic salons of early-twentieth-century Lima. Such miscegenation was anathema to the scientific racialism of the nineteenth century, however. Because scientific racialist thinkers believed that each race constituted a distinct and separate species, and hybrids were known in nature to be incapable of reproducing, many held that miscegenation led to infertility. Since this belief in the infertility of the multiracial individual contradicted reality, racialists proposed that hybrid populations became infertile only after several generations of continued miscegenation (Young 1995, 16). It was also held that miscegenation led to the degeneration of any beneficial qualities present in the original races (Young 1995, 16). As we have seen, given its racial plurality, Latin America became the privileged example of the supposed evils of miscegenation, as theorized by these "scientific" thinkers. The following statement about Brazil by Louis Agassiz, professor of zoology at Harvard, former protégé of Alexander von Humboldt and Louis Cuvier, and one of the most respected figures in nineteenth-century natural sciences, is paradigmatic of the evaluation of Latin America and of miscegenation by scientific racialism: "Let any one who doubts the evil of this mixture of races, and is inclined, from a mistaken philanthropy to break down all barriers between them, come to Brazil. He cannot deny the deterioration consequent upon the amalgamation of races more widespread here than any other country in the world, and which is rapidly effacing the best qualities of the white man, the Negro, and the Indian, leaving a mongrel nondescript type, deficient in physical and mental energy" (Agassiz and Agassiz 1886, 293). Therefore, scientific racialism considered the multiracial populations of Latin America to be inferior even to the races this pseudoscience classified as primitive—such as blacks and Indians.

The reaction of Latin American elites to scientific racialism was complex. On the one hand, scientific racialism provided a ready-made explanation for the social and economic failures of Latin America during the nineteenth century, which the elites could ascribe to the presence of black, Amerindian, and mixed-race populations. Moreover, by declaring themselves to be white, the Latin American oligarchies could claim a scientific justification for their exploitation of the darker-skinned, and supposedly inferior, Indian, black, and mixed-race masses. Seen from the perspective of scientific racialism, the inequality between the "white" elites and the "dark" majority—one of the characteristics of Latin America in the nineteenth century (and beyond)—became a natural and unavoidable social condition. Moreover, scientific racialism was fully congruent with the notion of an opposition between "civilization"—associated with the putatively white urban elites—and "barbarism"—represented by the mostly mestizo, Indian, and black rural populations—originally proposed by Argentinean intellectual Domingo Faustino Sarmiento.[9] The spread of scientific racialism, therefore, reinforced the separation, even opposition, between the putatively white national elites and the dark majority of the population.

There was, however, another side to scientific racialism that could not easily be assimilated by the Latin American elites. Scientific racialism, through its pessimistic evaluation of the consequences of miscegenation and its belief in the inferiority of nonwhite races, condemned the Latin American nations to occupy permanently subordinate positions in relation to Europe and the United States. The Mexican-American War, justified in the U.S. press on racialist grounds, exemplified from a Latin American perspective the dangerous uses that could be made of this new "scientific" point of view (Horsman 1981, 208–15). Moreover, since the "whiteness" of Latin American elites was often more fiction than fact, those elites were consequently positioned by scientific racialism as inferior to European and U.S. whites.

Influenced by scientific racialism, Latin American elites attempted to "whiten" their national populations. This concern with "improving" national racial stocks informed two complementary social measures: the extermination of supposedly inferior populations and the promotion of European immigration. Although the extermination of Amerindian populations already had a long history that dated back to the conquest, racialism provided an added justification for their annihilation. For instance, it is not accidental that in Argentina the so-called Conquest of the Desert, the war of extermination waged against the Indians, was begun in 1879, during the heyday of racialism (Helg 1990, 44).

Central to the different national elites' attempts to "whiten" the population of Latin American countries was the promotion of immigration from Europe. Not only was the influx of a putatively superior white population seen as beneficial to the nation, but a secondary goal was for large numbers of European immigrants to intermarry with the "dark" native populations—even though this contradicted scientific racialist theory. The two aspects of the elites' attempts to whiten the Latin American racial makeup—namely, annihilation and immigration—did not contradict each other. In fact, it was the genocide of the Amerindian population in Argentina that opened up the countryside to agriculture and lured European immigrants who were predominantly farmers (Helg 1990, 44).

In other Latin American countries the number of immigrants fell short of the expectations of the elites, and the hopes for a massive miscegenation of white immigrants with blacks, Amerindians, mestizos, and mulattoes did not materialize. (This was true even in Brazil, which received a sizable number of immigrants—3.5 million).[10]

Given this failure of whitening as a project to "improve" the predominantly mestizo, black, and Amerindian Latin American population, it became necessary to fashion a new response to the problems of race and nation. By the first decades of the twentieth century, Latin American intellectuals began to propose that mestizaje be viewed not as a flaw to be corrected by immigration, but as a characteristic that would define the nation as such.[11]

From Racialism to Mestizaje as the Basis of Nationhood

The appropriation of the word and concept of mestizaje to denote a positive process by which the national populations of Latin American countries, and of Latin America as a whole, would become constituted as a specific "race" and culture entailed a modification of the word's connotations. "Mestizaje" and "mestizo" derive from an older Spanish word *mesto,* which in turn originated from the Latin *mixtus,* used in agriculture to denote several types of hybrid plants (Moliner [1966] 1990, 402). Mestizo was used in agriculture and animal husbandry to name a hybrid animal or plant (Moliner [1966] 1990, 402). It is only during the establishment of the Spanish viceroyalties in the Americas that "mestizo" and "mestizaje" were extended to the new populations that arose out of sexual relationships between Spanish conquistadors and Indian women. Because mestizos and mulattoes were frequently born out of wedlock, the colonial authorities looked down on them, and the places they could live and the jobs they could hold were severely restricted (Álvarez 1978, 967).[12] To use mestizaje in a positive national context required not only rejecting the dogmas of scientific racialism, but also disregarding the negative connotations and uses that had been associated with the word and its cognates in Spanish. In fact, the verb *mestizar* is still defined as to "adulterate the purity of a race by crossing it with others" (Moliner [1966] 1990, 402), a meaning fully compatible with racialism.

Within the Latin American context, then, mestizaje acquires meanings that are very different from those attached to miscegenation. If miscegenation was seen as leading to the degeneration of the species and to infertility, mestizaje became (as a concept, if not in practice) the means through which to imagine the construction of a unified nation. Mestizaje permitted Latin American thinkers to claim for their countries the racial unity of a nation as conceived of in European thought. Mestizaje or, better said, the discourse of mestizaje, thus became a way for the three numerically dominant races living in the Americas—white, Amerindian, and black—to become incorporated into the same national project: they would commingle to form a new mestizo race, in which the constitutive qualities of each original race would contribute to and form a new and different whole. Since such a fusion was only partial—a fact evidenced by the ostensible persistence of separate and distinct races in Latin America—nationality became a project only incompletely achieved, bound to become fully realized in the future as the "coexistence and crossing of the races" progressed (Riva Agüero 1955, 117). The discourse of mestizaje thus stands, in some respects, in profound opposition to scientific racialism: where racialism saw degeneration, the discourse of mestizaje saw development and national consolidation; where racialism saw the national failure of the Latin American states, the discourse of mestizaje saw the grounding possibility of the nation as such.

Nevertheless, despite the tenets that clearly situated the discourse of mestizaje as opposing racialism, it can also be understood as a continuation of scientific racialism. The discourse of mestizaje, particularly in its earlier versions, still maintained the idea of race as central to its proposals, and assigned permanent and hereditary characteristics to each race. In fact, not only are the characteristics assigned by the proponents of mestizaje to blacks, Amerindians, whites, and on occasion Asians, reminiscent of the stereotypes present in racialist writings, but frequently the same racial hierarchy is maintained.[13]

It is not accidental that the discourse of mestizaje became an important national and regional ideology in the early twentieth century, precisely the period when criticism of the doctrines of scientific racialism began not only in Europe and the United States, but also in Latin America. Starting in the late nineteenth century, Latin American intellectuals such as the Peruvian Manuel González Prada and the Brazilian Manoel Bomfim emphasized the nonscientific and imperialist nature of racialism, thus helping to create an intellectual climate less dominated by the dogmas of this pseudoscience.[14]

Moreover, around the end of the nineteenth century, culture slowly began to replace race as the principal classificatory concept of human difference. Because this process was far from concluded when the first writings proposing mestizaje as the basis for Latin American nationalities were produced, there is a confusion of race and culture in these works. Since both race and culture are markers of difference, however, there is already conceptual overlap between them. Thus, mestizaje became not only a racial but also a cultural concept. In the cultural version of the discourse of mestizaje, the fusion is not seen as necessarily or even primarily biological, but rather as cultural: out of the interrelationships among Amerindians, Spaniards or Portuguese, and blacks, a new national culture is arising that retains what is of value in each of its three constitutive cultural traditions.

Just as race and culture overlap, cultural and racial versions of the discourse of mestizaje have in practice tended to blend into one another. The writings of Peruvian historian José de la Riva Agüero during the 1910s and 1920s illustrate the difficulty that proponents of the discourse of mestizaje encounter in separating concepts of race and culture. In his *Paisajes peruanos*, he prefaces his description of the "Indian race" as follows: "If there is a truth proven by history, it is that the human races do not possess immutable psychological traits, but instead have tendencies that lead to diverse results according to circumstance" (Riva Agüero 1955, 187). Rather than writing about the inheritance of fixed and specific genetic traits, which are central to any true racial thinking, Riva Agüero writes about tendencies that result in an unpredictable array of attitudes and behaviors. In his formulation, the concept of race has lost any descriptive or predictive value. Therefore, his description of the customs, attitudes, and traditions of the "Indian race" can be read as much as an analysis of culture as of race. There is also a frequent slippage from the concept of culture back to that of race among proponents of cultural variants of the discourse of mestizaje. For instance, José Carlos Mariátegui, who throughout his works declares race invalid as an analytical concept, frequently resorts to racial stereotypes in his descriptions of human behavior.[15]

In many Latin American texts that attempt to use mestizaje to define the nation, the slippage back and forth between culture and race remains a constant. Definitions of nationality that seem to propose racial versions of mestizaje frequently define racial characteristics as dependent on environmental, including cultural, factors. On the other hand, proponents of cultural mestizaje frequently resort to racial stereotypes. Therefore, in the Latin American discourse of mestizaje the distinction between racial and cultural versions tends to blur. Nevertheless, the ambiguity present in the terms used to define the nation is a weakness only from a critical perspective. If these texts are analyzed as national projects—that is, as texts that attempt to provide a definition of the nation with which their diverse readers can identify—this ambiguity can be taken as a strength. In the twentieth century, Latin American nations have been founded discursively around an ambiguity between culture and race. Since racial and cultural versions of the discourse of mestizaje are frequently indistinguishable, this ambiguity provides intellectuals with a common language and even, at least on the surface, a common perspective regardless whether they propose a cultural or a racial version. The similarities between these variants are, after all, much greater than their differences: in both versions of the discourse of mestizaje, the reality of racial and cultural heterogeneity is reconciled with a unitary conceptualization of the nation that reproduces the European formula for nationality. Thus the discourse of mestizaje lends itself to widely variant interpretations—from racial to cultural, from politically conservative to Marxist, from discriminatory to egalitarian. The polysemous nature of the concept of mestizaje creates a common semantic field in which discourse about the nation can be grounded. The fact that the discourse of mestizaje informs the works of conservatives such as José de la Riva Agüero, radicals such as José Vasconcelos of the 1920s, and Marxists such as José Carlos Mariátegui exemplifies the success of the concept. In Latin America, the discourse of mestizaje established the parameters within which different political and ideological proposals were made, because until recently it provided the only way to conceptualize the creation of a unitary nation from a heterogeneous population. The plasticity of this discourse—the ease with which it can be molded to fit conservative, liberal, and radical ideologies—explains its hegemony in Latin America by the 1920s.[16] It is only when the notion of a unitary race or culture as a precondition for the conceptualization and constitution of a nation—or the nation itself—is questioned that it becomes possible for Latin Americans to propose alternative forms of identity.

The discourse of mestizaje, in both its cultural and racial variants, is problematic in another sense. Although it proposes to ground the nation in either a racial or cultural unity that can be achieved by the fusion of the white, Amerindian, and black populations, the "national culture" is in fact defined as corresponding to that of the ruling criollo classes. In spite of the discussion about cultural or racial fusion, there is no doubt in the minds of many of the proponents of the discourse of mestizaje that Spanish is the nation's language and, in the writings of the more conservative, Catholicism its religion. Thus, mestizaje can be seen as a kind of assimilationism.

The fact that the national culture is implicitly identified with that of the elites has led some critics to claim that the discourse of mestizaje is simply a facade that permits the oppression of Amerindian and black groups under the banner of their incorporation into the national community, that is, a cover-up for ethnocide (Kahn 1995, 19). For these critics, cultural or racial versions of the discourse of mestizaje permit the elites to talk about a nation common to all ethnic groups while continuing to exploit the Amerindian and black populations. Moreover, since the best features of Amerindian and black cultures are claimed already to have been incorporated, or to be in the process of being incorporated, into the national culture, the discourse of mestizaje can be used to justify the destruction of these cultures. In other words, since the nation is formed by the incorporation of Amerindian and black "races" or cultures into the criollo "mainstream," mestizaje is practically identical to a process of acculturation. Moreover, by rhetorically claiming that the best features of these "oppressed" cultures have been or are being incorporated into the "national culture," the discourse of mestizaje eliminates much of the intellectual justification for Amerindian or black resistance to that culture.

The success of the discourse of mestizaje as a national ideology is far from accidental. From colonial times until the wars of independence, it had been customary for the criollo elites to use the figure of the Amerindian as a symbol of an identity separate and different from that of the metropolis in terms that clearly prefigured the discourse of mestizaje. Octavio Paz writes about this use of the figure of the Amerindian by the criollos of New Spain:

> In the seventeenth century criollo identity—to avoid the equivocal word "nationalism"—was expressed in artistic creation and philosophical and religious speculations in which the image of New Spain appears, more or less veiled, as the Other Spain. With some confusion, the criollo felt he was heir to two empires, Spanish and Indian.

With the same contradictory fervor with which he exalted the Hispanic Empire and detested the Spanish, he glorified the Indian past and disdained the Indians. (Paz 1988, 36)

In this quotation, Paz establishes certain peculiarities about the use of the figure of the Amerindian by the colonial criollo elites. On the one hand, by asserting their rhetorical community with the Amerindian, the colonial elites created a discourse of American difference from Spain. The criollos could see themselves as "other" from Spain, as Paz points out. Moreover, it must be remembered that the Amerindian is not only an autochthonous presence in the Americas, but also a figure of resistance to Spain. Therefore by presenting themselves as inheritors of the Amerindian cultures, the criollo elites managed to give historical density to their desire for autonomy and, later, independence. Not surprisingly, this rhetorical fraternity with the Amerindian reached a climax during the struggle for independence. Probably the most famous literary example of this imaginary continuity between the Amerindian and the nineteenth-century criollo is José Joaquín de Olmedo's "La victoria de Junín" (1825). In it the Inca Huayna Capac addresses Simón Bolívar, the triumphant leader of the struggle for independence, as "son and friend and avenger of the Inca," and the new Latin American nations as "peoples that form one single people and family and are all my children" (Olmedo 1979, 20). Although the identification with the Spanish Empire is not present in Olmedo's poem, as it was for the colonial criollos described by Paz, the figure of the Amerindian is still central to the assertion of independence from Spain. Needless to say, as is implied in the quotation from Paz, this identification with the Amerindian did not affect the hierarchical relations between criollos and Indians. It did, however, leave a significant imprint on Latin American literature, perhaps most importantly on two central nineteenth-century writers: the Peruvian Ricardo Palma (1833–1919) and the Brazilian novelist José de Alencar (1829–1877), who anticipate in their literary work much of the discourse of mestizaje, which would not become fully articulated until around the turn of the century.

Thus the discourse of mestizaje is in many ways a continuation of an earlier criollo rhetorical tradition. Although the theorists of both cultural and racial variants claim to ground their reflections on what were then the latest trends in Western scientific thought (e.g., Riva Agüero on positivism, Mariátegui on Marxism) the Amerindian frequently continues to serve as a historical origin for the nation. That is, by discursively incorporating the Amerindian into the nation, the discourse of mestizaje makes it possible to claim for the national society a history independent from that of Spain or Portugal.

However, there are limits to the capacity of the discourse of mestizaje to accept difference. For example, since language is generally seen as central to the definition of the nation, linguistic difference is frequently considered to be inassimilable. The emphasis put on teaching Spanish to Amerindian groups in Spanish America illustrates the degree to which linguistic difference is seen as a threat to national unity. In fact, the promotion of Spanish literacy among Amerindians was proposed in the Congreso Indigenista Interamericano in Pátzcuaro, Mexico, in 1940 not only as an official national goal for the different Latin American countries, but as the most urgent measure to be undertaken on behalf of the Amerindians. Although framed originally as an attempt to help the Amerindians of the Americas, the resolutions of the congress were fully congruent with the ideology of the discourse of mestizaje, which proposes the integration of the Amerindian populations into their respective national societies rather than the preservation of their cultures. Not surprisingly, the measures proposed by the congress were quickly ratified by the countries with large Amerindian populations: Mexico (1941), Ecuador (1942), Peru (1943), and Bolivia (1945) (Saintoul 1988, 20).

Parallels between Mestizaje and U.S. Multiculturalism

Although the United States, like Latin America, has always been characterized by the racial and cultural heterogeneity of its population, the concern with incorporating its nonwhite population into conceptualizations of the nation is a recent phenomenon. The melting pot permitted the incorporation of European immigrants, who constituted the great majority of the population, into the nation. But the numerical growth and politicization of minorities as well as their partial incorporation into positions of leadership in the nation as a whole from the 1960s on has led to the production of new versions of the nation that take into account this cultural and ethnic diversity. Thus the emergence of the concept of multiculturalism in the United States in the 1980s and 1990s echoes in numerous ways the discussions surrounding mestizaje in Latin America that began in the 1920s, if not before. After all, both the discourse of mestizaje and multiculturalism are attempts at coping with the cultural, racial, and ethnic heterogeneity present in American societies.

However, unlike the situation in Latin America, the rise of multiculturalism in the United States is directly related to a change in the composition of the intellectual and political elites of the country. (It is much more difficult to argue that there has been a parallel change in the economic elites.) In its different variants, multiculturalism bears traces of the Civil Rights struggle of the 1960s. Whether multicultural proposals attempt to continue that period's emphasis on race or not, they are all marked by, indeed are a consequence of, the denuding of the limitations of the implicitly white assimilationism of the melting pot that resulted from the Civil Rights Movement.

Multiculturalism as an attempt at coming to grips with the progressive hybridization of the culture and population of the United States can thus be described as an example of the "Latinization" of the country (Stam 1997, 15). The problematics of the discourse of mestizaje are, therefore, no longer relevant exclusively to Latin America but have acquired continent-wide importance. Moreover, it is because American writers, in the hemispheric sense of the word, have had to face the problem of reconciling national identity with a heterogeneous reality that it becomes possible to find an affinity among the diverse literary traditions of the Americas. Mestizaje and multiculturalism are ultimately the names for an American commonality that does not deny regional and national difference, but rather finds a common ground for the literary, critical, and theoretical writings of the continent.

CHAPTER THREE

Ricardo Palma's

Tradiciones peruanas

The Limits of the Discourse of Mestizaje

If the defeat of the Spanish colonial armies in the battle of Ayacucho (1824) marked the moment when political independence was finally achieved in Peru and in Spanish America as a whole, the corresponding cultural and intellectual autonomy was to prove more elusive. The difficulty inherent in the creation of an autonomous national project in countries that had been politically and culturally dependent on the Spanish metropolis was greater in the case of Peru. The country had been for most of the colonial period the political and cultural center of Spanish South America, and Spanish mores and cultural patterns were deeply ingrained in the country's elite.[1] Moreover, Peru's first two decades of independence were marked by political and military unrest. It was only in the 1840s that the political stability needed for the development of a sustained literary and intellectual production was finally achieved in the country.[2]

Ricardo Palma, the first major author of independent Peru, describes the work of the writers of this period of political consolidation as focusing on the development of a cultural independence from Spain: "I belonged to the small group of writers of Peru after the country's independence. Born under the shadow of the republic's flag, it was our obligation to break with the mannerisms of colonial writers, and we boldly set out to fulfill this enterprise. And as soldiers of a new and passionate generation, we, the bohemian revolutionaries, fought with faith and with success, from 1848 to 1860" (Palma 1953, 1321). Palma's laudatory words exaggerate the achievements of his contemporaries, since elsewhere in his memoirs, "La bohemia de mi tiempo" (1899), his evaluation of their work is much less enthusiastic (see pp. 1298, 1300, 1302, 1303, 1321). However, this statement is significant because it compares these early writers of postcolonial Peru with the armies that had previously achieved independence in the battlefields (for example, the writers are described as "soldiers," "revolutionaries," etc.). Despite his rather modest description of what these writers actually accomplished—Palma praises them merely for breaking with colonial literary mannerisms—the comparison itself alludes to the much greater feat of achieving literary and even cultural independence from Spain. We might use these words of Palma's to describe his own *Tradiciones peruanas* (1872–1915), the most important work produced in that literary generation.[3] Palma's *Tradiciones peruanas* can be read as the most significant attempt by any member of this generation of "literary soldiers" to achieve independence from Spanish literary and cultural models.

The creation of national literatures and identities independent of Spain was particularly difficult in Spanish America. Criollo Spanish Americans were clearly the linguistic, cultural, racial, and even administrative inheritors of the Spanish Empire. (The new countries roughly followed the boundaries of the colonial viceroyalties and captainships.) The profound links between the criollos and Spain explain the need felt by Spanish American writers to find a cultural source that would not be subordinated to that of the metropolis; and, as I discussed in chapter 2, since colonial times it had been in Amerindian history and culture that such an independent basis for identity had been found.

Nevertheless, with independence such foundational use of the Indian became more problematic—especially in the case of Peru. Since a majority of the Peruvian population was of indigenous origin, and Amerindian cultures were still a vital reality, any true national project had to deal explicitly with the manner in which the Amerindian was to be incorporated within the conceptualization of the nation. Indian presence and history were not only what differentiated Peru from other "national" cultures, but because of the Andean Indians' continuing cultural autonomy and physical isolation from the criollo coast, also an impediment to any Peruvian claim to nationhood. After all, national identity is predicated on the existence of a criterion—whether racial, linguistic, or cultural—according to which the population in question may be seen as internally homogeneous and at the same time distinct from its neighbors. Therefore, the problem faced by any Peruvian literary or political national project was to propose a conceptualization of the nation as homogeneous in spite of the cultural, linguistic, and to some extent racial divide between a coastal region "descended" from Spain and a predominantly Quechua and Aymara Indian Andean region. As a national text, Palma's *Tradiciones peruanas* had both to represent a Peru that was autonomous from Spain and, at the same time, to bridge the obvious cultural, linguistic, and racial divisions that threatened to tear the nation asunder.

There is a national dimension even in the formal features of *Tradiciones peruanas*. For instance, the work deviates from colonial literary mannerisms at the level of genre. By inventing a new genre—the *tradición* itself—Palma reaffirms in formal literary terms the country's independence from Spain. Palma's creation of the tradición implied that colonial genres were no longer capable of representing an independent Spanish America. A new American genre was required to adequately represent a new American reality.

Technically, thematically, and perhaps also linguistically heterogeneous, the tradición is a genre that defies precise definition. Although some of Palma's tradiciones are written in verse, most are written in prose and are similar to short stories; still others, also in prose, are more akin to essays. Although because of this heterogeneity the tradiciones cannot be subsumed by conventional definitions, for our purposes they can be described as brief, usually humorous, prose narratives that explain the origins of words and proverbs or narrate obscure historical facts.[4] Palma's tradiciones are concerned with the origin of Peruvian and American identity and difference. Paradoxically, the culturally heterogeneous origins of these narratives (they are of Indian, Spanish, criollo, and black provenance) are used in the *Tradiciones peruanas* to establish the necessarily homogeneous Peruvian, and even regional, frame.

Palma's title alone reveals much about the text's thematic focus and contexts. His work is not only characterized by its historical subject matter, but this history is described as being both plural—tradiciones not tradición—and Peruvian. The *Tradiciones peruanas* assume the cultural and ethnic plurality that characterizes both Peru and Latin America in order to propose a national identity that subsumes this plurality. Therefore, the apparent cultural plurality of the *Tradiciones peruanas* does not contradict the creation of a unitary and homogeneous national history and identity. On the contrary, in a frequent gesture of the discourse of mestizaje, Palma represents Peruvian and American history as beginning not with the colonial period but with the Indian past. Moreover, the republic is presented not only as descended from both Incan and colonial pasts, but also as a later stage in Peru's development when these contradictory moments in the nation's history—as well as the Amerindian and Spanish populations hegemonic during those periods—are at least potentially reconciled. Palma's representation of the nation in the *Tradiciones peruanas* thereby prefigures the later theorizations of mestizaje.

Like the theoretical discourse of mestizaje of the early twentieth century, Palma's work presents the nation as based on the fusion and reconciliation of the Spanish and Amerindian populations and their cultural elements. Palma's affinity with the later versions of the discourse of mestizaje was implicitly acknowledged by Peruvian historian and early proponent of mestizaje José de la Riva Agüero. During Palma's later years, in a 1912 ceremony in honor of the *tradicionista,* Riva Agüero (1962, 359) described him as "one of the principal and most efficient agents in the formation of our nationality." Later critics have echoed Riva Agüero's characterization of Palma as a central figure in the building of an independent national identity in Peru and have discerned his influence in other parts of Spanish America (see Rodríguez-Arenas 1993, 381; Unzueta 1993, 503–4).

El Corregidor de Tinta

Among his tradiciones, "El corregidor de Tinta," first published in 1874, demonstrates best how Palma's conceptualization of the nation incorporated Indian history and populations. This tradición narrates the failed revolt against Spanish authority that took place in 1780–81 under the leadership of an Inca noble, José Gabriel Condorcanqui, better known as Tupac Amaru II. The rebellion concluded with the death by dismemberment of Tupac Amaru and the torture and execution of his family. Generally acknowledged by historians as the most significant of all Indian rebellions, its scope was such that, as Palma (1953, 687) writes, "Independence was almost achieved."

When Palma identifies the goals of Tupac Amaru's rebellion with the struggle for independence of his criollo "successors," he clearly equates the Indian leader with the later revolutionaries. Moreover, the description of Tupac Amaru II emphasizes his assimilation of criollo/European manners and customs, since he is described as knowledgeable about the rules of etiquette appropriate to a meal celebrating the birthday of the Spanish King Carlos III. In fact, Palma contrasts the behavior of the "noble Indian," as he calls Tupac Amaru, with the crass conduct of the noble-by-birth Spanish functionary Antonio Arriaga, who takes the revolutionary's seat at the table during the celebration (p. 685). Ironically, it is the Indian who is shown as exemplifying European standards of courtesy and nobility by graciously ignoring Arriaga's rudeness, while the Spaniard is presented as willfully breaking them.

While "El corregidor de Tinta" identifies the exploitation of the Amerindians as one of the causes of Tupac Amaru's rebellion, the tradición also emphasizes the negative effect on the rest of the Peruvian population of Arriaga's abuses and, by extension, the Spanish colonial despotism that makes the actions of the corregidor possible (p. 685).[5] "El corregidor de Tinta" situates not the Indian, but the Spanish colonial authorities as an "outside" element with respect to the nation. Arriaga is cast as an extraneous element that imposes itself on a community that, in its multiethnic and multiracial composition, seems to figure the Peruvian population. Thus, the rebels who begin the revolt by executing the "foreign" functionary Arriaga include Indians, blacks, criollos, and perhaps even Spanish settlers—since these are the peoples who are described as having been exploited by Arriaga (p. 686).[6] This tradición not only incorporates Indians and blacks within its representation of the nation; it also assigns to Amerindians, through the figure of Tupac Amaru, and to blacks, through the figure of Arriaga's slave (who is his master's executioner), a central role in national history. Although "El corregidor de Tinta" presents detailed information about the racial or national origin only of Tupac Amaru, Arriaga, and the black slave, the figure of a table around which the "national" elements participate as equals (Indians, criollos, and perhaps also some Spaniards) can be taken as representative of the conceptualization of the nation implicit in Palma's *Tradiciones peruanas*. This deeply democratic representation of the different ethnic and racial groups that make up Peru is characteristic of many of Palma's tradiciones. Although the description of Tupac Amaru as not only participating in national society but actually becoming its representative and leader reflects the heroic dimension of the character, throughout Palma's *Tradiciones peruanas* other less exalted Amerindian and black characters are also presented as participants in an egalitarian representation of the nation.[7]

However, the democratic representation of the nation in "El corregidor de Tinta" is based on a refusal to address the central problem faced by any conceptualization of the Peruvian nation: the existence of a profound cultural, linguistic, and racial division between the criollo coast and the Indian Andes. In this tradición, Palma achieves an egalitarian representation of Peru by ignoring the social and racial inequalities and linguistic and cultural divisions that in reality threatened the nation. For instance, though Tupac Amaru's rebellion was an Amerindian movement, in the tradición it is not identified as such. Tupac Amaru, after all, did not attempt to found a criollo republic, but rather aimed to re-establish the Inca Empire, or at least a modified version of it. Moreover, Palma's egalitarian representation is in profound contradiction to the reality of the criollos' exploitation of and discrimination against Indians and blacks.

In order to produce a verisimilar representation of Peru, Palma would have had to address the bicultural and bilingual reality that not only differentiated the country from the former metropolis, but also threatened its constitution as a nation. Therefore, any version of the discourse of mestizaje in Peru must be capable of (at least rhetorically) reconciling the existence of a dual cultural and linguistic tradition (Indian and Spanish/criollo) with a homogeneous conception of the nation.

Carta Canta

The tradición that addresses the bicultural problem most fully is "Carta canta" (1875). However, the simultaneous representation of the Indian as the origin of national difference and of the exploitation of the Indian as the economic basis of the nation lead this tradición to collapse into a series of contradictory statements and positions. But since the reconciliation of the rhetorically privileged position of the Indian as the ostensible originator of the nation with the actual exploitation of the Amerindian population is one of the central problems faced by the discourse of mestizaje, the analysis of "Carta canta" is central to the analysis of this discourse as a whole.

"Carta canta" gains additional significance in that it is possible (at least in part) to identify the narrator with Ricardo Palma. The tradición is presented as a lexicological investigation into the origins of the saying *carta canta* (letter sings/tells) that gives the text its name. Not only was Palma notable for his interest in the origins of American and Peruvian sayings and words, as illustrated by his well-known essay "Neologismos y americanismos" (1895), but he actually proposed that "carta canta" be included in the Diccionario de la Real Academia de la Lengua, as a *peruanismo* (Chang-Rodríguez 1971, 434).

"Carta canta" narrates a story different versions of which appear in several of the *crónicas* (historical narratives of the conquest).[8] In Palma's version, two Indian workers on the conquistador Antonio Solar's *encomienda* are ordered by an overseer to take ten melons and a letter to the conquistador in Lima.[9] The Indians, for whom this fruit is a novelty, decide to taste it and stop on the road to eat two of the melons. Since they believe that the letter is capable of reporting on their actions, the Indians place the letter behind a fence so that their actions are hidden from it. When they arrive at Solar's house, they give him the remaining melons, but when he reads the letter he realizes that two are missing. He then punishes the Indians, who in response to their beating exclaim, "carta canta." Solar hears the phrase and repeats it to his friends. In time the Indians' exclamation becomes a saying known throughout the Spanish-speaking world.

Since "Carta canta" is presented primarily as a lexicological investigation, one might attempt to connect the linguistic aspects of the text with the concern in the *Tradiciones peruanas* for creating a unified conceptualization of the Peruvian nation. In *Escribir en el aire* (1994), Antonio Cornejo Polar has followed precisely this analytical path in a suggestive study that rightly emphasizes the manner in which this text manages to create a homogeneous representation of the heterogeneous and divided reality of Peru. For him, it is through the analysis of the linguistic aspects of "Carta canta" that it is possible to discern how this tradición "produces a linguistic space . . . pleasant, almost paradisiacal, where the nation can read itself—without conflicts as such" (Cornejo Polar 1994, 12).

In his analysis Cornejo Polar emphasizes the subtle movement from Quechua to Spanish that, according to Palma, characterizes the development of the phrase "carta canta." He points out that at the beginning of the story, when the Indians decide to eat the melons, it is clearly stated that they speak in "indigenous dialect"—that is, Quechua (p. 148). Nevertheless, the tradición concludes with the Indians speaking in the conquistadors' language and originating a Spanish saying: "carta canta"

(p. 148). Cornejo Polar argues that "in this manner, there is an almost imperceptible displacement from Quechua to Spanish, and the correlated erasure of the former" (p. 109). According to this analysis, the specifically Amerindian cultural and linguistic difference, which is the source of the phrase "carta canta," is transmuted into a general and homogeneous "national" difference once the saying is incorporated into the "national" language, Spanish.[10]

However, the erasure of Quechua and its replacement by Spanish can, according to Cornejo Polar, also be read as implying the existence of a linguistic hierarchy in which the European language is situated above that of the Indians. In "Carta canta," this implied hierarchy is evidenced by the narrator's use of the information provided in the tradición as historical support to claim before the Academia de la Lengua in Madrid that the phrase "carta canta" is of Peruvian origin—which Palma in fact did. According to Cornejo Polar, it is thus possible to see in "Carta canta" a process by which "Quechua submits to Spanish, oral to written language, and all to the authority of the [Royal Language] Academy" (p. 110). In Cornejo Polar's analysis, the linguistic is a sign for the social. Therefore, the presence of a linguistic hierarchy implies that the national homogeneity achieved in "Carta canta," and the *Tradiciones peruanas* as a whole, is characterized by the existence of a hierarchy in which the criollos occupy a position superior to that of the Indians (p. 112).

This analysis is not only the most complete study attempted of this tradición,[11] but in its paradoxes, Cornejo Polar's text reflects the contradictions and ambiguity that characterize "Carta canta" itself. For Cornejo Polar, "Carta canta" figures the elimination of the cultural, racial, and linguistic divisions of the country through the subordination of the Amerindians to the criollos. The validation of this homogeneous version of the nation is, paradoxically, described by Cornejo Polar as resting at least partly in Spain (as represented by the authority of the Real Academia de la Lengua). In this analysis, homogeneity is achieved through a reinstatement of the cultural subordination of the nation to Spain. Therefore, in "Carta canta" Palma would appear to have betrayed the search for cultural independence, which is in fact one of the underlying aims of the *Tradiciones peruanas*. Given that Cornejo Polar argues that "Carta canta" presents Peru as hierarchically structured, with the Indians positioned as inferior to the criollos and Spaniards, he seems to contradict his own reading, which finds in this tradición a description of the nation as a virtual paradise. After all, what kind of paradise is founded on inequality?

However, "Carta canta" can also be read, as Cornejo Polar briefly observes, as part of "a just process of vindication of *americanismos*" (p. 110). One can argue that Palma's text not only valorizes the words and phrases that originally derive from Peru and America, but also presents a claim that the Spanish language is no longer exclusively Iberian in origin. "Carta canta," as well as the *Tradiciones peruanas* as a whole, can be read as an attempt to "nationalize" (from a Peruvian and Spanish American perspective) the Spanish language; that is, as part of a project to make the use of the language of the metropolis compatible with the claims for national and continental independence so dear to Palma and his generation. If language and nation are intertwined in nineteenth-century thought, the attempt to nationalize the Spanish language is a necessary part of any Spanish American national project. Even the reference to the Real Academia de la Lengua (in the tradición and in Palma's real-life linguistic proposal) is not necessarily incompatible with national independence, since Palma's conception of the role of the Real Academia de la Lengua was extremely democratic—he stresses the sovereignty of popular use and the positioning of all the Spanish-speaking nations on an equal plane.[12]

There is nonetheless an ambiguity contained within the national project that is virtually put forth in this tradición. This ambiguity originates in the complex nature of Spanish American national identity and especially in the way that such identity was proposed in the nineteenth century. It was—and occasionally still is—common for a national identity to be complemented with a continental (Latin) American one. But especially in the nineteenth century, a Hispanic identity manifested in a strong sense of connection to and identification with Spain was also common, even among writers such as Palma, whose work was centered precisely on the development of an independent national project. However, Palma's staunch support of Peruvian independence is manifested in his historical study of his generation, "La bohemia de mi tiempo" (1899), in the tradición "El corregidor de Tinta" (1874), as well as in numerous other texts, which stand as proof of his unflagging devotion to an autonomous and independent Peru and Latin America. Nevertheless, the tension between the sense of identification with Spain and the desire for national autonomy

can be taken as a sign of the contradictory relationship between the criollos' attempt to establish a national identity independent from Spain and
their position as the linguistic, cultural, and even economic inheritors of
the colony.

While one can read "Carta canta" as figuring the displacement of
Quechua by Spanish, it is also possible to see a different relation between
these languages staged in this tradición. In fact, it is impossible to know
which language is used in the discursive exchange between Aguilar and
the two Indians. (The text does not indicate whether the Indians speak
Spanish or Aguilar understands Quechua.) However, what is relevant is
not the language spoken by the Indians, but rather that the tradición
presents a situation in which there is a fluid flow of information between
two radically dissimilar cultural and linguistic groups: the Spaniards and
the Quechua Indians. "Carta canta," therefore, can be read as presenting a
narrative world characterized by perfect translatability. If, like Cornejo
Polar, one can claim for "Carta canta," and for the *Tradiciones peruanas* as a
whole, the status of a linguistic utopia, such a utopia exists precisely in the
possibility of words and phrases moving from Quechua to Spanish and, in
principle, from Spanish to Quechua without any loss of meaning. It is the
possibility of words and, by extension, cultural products moving from the
Amerindian to the criollo poles of the Peruvian nation that legitimates the
use of the Indian as an origin of national difference. The fiction of perfect
translatability permits the purportedly mestizo culture of the criollos to be
posited as the inheritor of what is best in Indian traditions and culture.
The criollos can therefore present themselves as descendants of the Indian
cultures, not as their destroyers. The lexicological story narrated in "Carta
canta" exemplifies the process by which Indian culture and language are
appropriated by the criollo elites as a source of national specificity: the
phrase "carta canta" originates among the Amerindians; is quickly incorporated by the conquistadors who, following Cornejo Polar, can be taken
as representing criollo society; and finally becomes both a Peruvian contribution to the Spanish language and, as a peruanismo, a sign of national
difference.

In "Carta canta," however, both the emphasis on the role of the
Indian as the origin of national difference and the fiction of perfect translatability, which makes such use of the Indian language and culture possible, are based on the suppression of a crucial fact implicit in the diegesis
but never made explicit by the narrator: the meaning of the phrase "carta

canta" is not the same throughout the tradición. For the Indians in "Carta canta," written language has magical qualities: "They believed that letters were not conventional signs, but spirits that not only functioned as messengers, but also as lookouts or spies" (Palma 1953, 148). When the Indians create the saying "carta canta," they are referring to what they believe to be the supernatural power of written language and reaffirming a magical worldview. The narrator and his contemporaries use the phrase "carta canta" with a completely different meaning, however: "with the meaning that this or that fact is mentioned in letters" (p. 146). Thus for the narrator and his readers, the phrase "carta canta" is a reaffirmation of the superior precision of writing over the vagaries of the spoken word. Moreover, whereas for the Indians the magical properties of the written word permit what is written to change according to circumstance, the narrator's interpretation insists on the inalterability of writing.

Mediating between both meanings of the phrase is the figure of the conquistador Solar. His first use of the phrase reaffirms its actual meaning but uses the magical interpretation of writing implicit in the phrase for his own benefit. Addressing the Indians, who after their punishment have exclaimed "carta canta," Aguilar exclaims: "Rogues, beware of doing it again. Now you know that the letter tells" (p. 148). Solar uses the Indians' belief in the magical properties of writing as a means of social control. He takes an aspect of Indian culture and uses it to acquire power over them. The Indians are admonished to follow the orders of the conquistador because the letter may inform him of any future disobedience. Yet Solar also originates the modern interpretation of the phrase: "And Don Antonio mentioned the case to his friends, and the saying became well known, even crossing the ocean" (p. 148). Through him the phrase spoken by the Indians becomes a saying known throughout the Spanish-speaking world, the affirmation of the magical mutability of the written word becomes a statement of its immutability. Solar's position in the origination of the phrase "carta canta" is thus ambiguous. Like the proverbial translator, he is both a conduit for the phrase from Quechua to Spanish and a manipulator of its meaning.

The representation of Solar and the conquistadors as a group in "Carta canta" is also ambiguous. If one concentrates on the descriptions of the conquistadors presented in the narrative, it is possible to read "Carta canta" as a critique of the conquest. Throughout the tradición, with Palma's characteristic subtlety and irony, the narrator emphasizes

Solar's and the conquistadors' oppressive role in the new colony. In five brief paragraphs, it is stated that Solar was rewarded with vast lands in spite of the fact that he arrived after the military conquest;[13] that the greed of the conquistadors led them to attempt to seize "lands as far as can be seen and got" (p. 147); and that, consistent with this description, the Indians interpreted the conquistadors' importation of oxen as another sign of their refusal to do any work themselves.[14] But the critique of the conquistadors is not limited to their laziness or greed. In fact, "Carta canta" portrays the colonial order as based on the exploitation of and violence against the Indian.

The representation of violence done to the Amerindian in "Carta canta" is framed, strangely enough, by a discourse of plenty that praises the fertility of American soil and the abundance of American agricultural production: "Some of the new seeds gave in Peru a larger and more abundant fruit than in Spain; . . . in the valley of Azapa, in Arica, a beet grew so large that a man could not put his arms around it" (p. 147). However, the narrator brings into sharp relief the difference between the effects of this fertility and plenty on the conquistadors and on the Indians. While for the Spaniards the fertility of the land is a source of wonder and, as the new owners of the land, wealth, the new produce is described as deadly to the Indians. Melons, lemons, apples, cherries, are all described— without any attempt at scientific or logical explanation—as killing the Indians who eat them in large numbers (p. 148). In fact, the pepino is singled out as being so deadly that "a century [after its introduction] . . . a bull was published that the priests read to their parishioners after Sunday mass prohibiting Indians from eating pepinos, a type of fruit called Indian killer because of its lethal effects" (p. 148).

But the violence against the Amerindian is not limited in "Carta canta" to the field of agriculture. Violence is implicit in the colonial legal institutions described in the tradición. Solar is described as an encomendero. Recall that the encomienda was a colonial institution under which Indians would work for a conquistador in exchange for instruction in the Christian faith. In practice, this institution was a form of slavery since it permitted the unrestricted exploitation of the Indian workforce. In "Carta canta," the violent nature of the encomienda is made clear when Solar punishes his Indian "wards" (p. 148). Moreover, by mentioning Solar's violent opposition to Viceroy Blasco Núñez de Vela's attempt at reforming the encomienda, Palma emphasizes the conquistador's refusal to accept the placement of any limits on his legal right to exploit the Indians (p. 147).[15]

"Carta canta," therefore, makes explicit the conquistadors' parasitic relation to Peruvian society. Indeed the only contribution attributed to them is the importation of new agricultural products, an achievement that, as we have seen, did not benefit the Indians. In fact, it is possible to read "Carta canta" as narrating two acts of stealing: that of the theft of the fruit by the Amerindians and that of the appropriation of America by the conquistadors, surely a more serious crime.[16] Thus "Carta canta" not only represents a virtually homogeneous national paradise but also emphasizes the class, racial, cultural, and economic divisions that have their origin in the Spanish conquest and colonization of Amerindian lands and peoples.

However, unlike earlier pro-Indian works, such Las Casas's *Brevísima relación de la destrucción de las Indias* (1542), or some of the later indigenista novels, such as César Vallejo's *El tungsteno* (1931) or Ciro Alegría's *El mundo es ancho y ajeno* (1941), "Carta canta" insinuates rather than represents the brutality of the oppression of the Indian. An example of the indirect representation of the conquistadors' genocide is the displacement of violence from the conquistadors to the European agricultural products they bring. And the central, even generative (since it originates the saying that is the subject of the text) moment of violence in "Carta canta," Solar's beating of the Indians, is not directly represented either: the narrator mentions the conquistador's decision to punish the Indians, then describes their conversation after this ordeal (p. 148).

Even the violence of the Indians' punishment, a clear example of the injustice of the colonial order, is itself diluted by the manner in which the Indian characters are represented. Their magical interpretation of writing and their inability to recognize Solar's manipulative use of their beliefs mark the two Indians as childlike characters, a fact emphasized in the tradición when they address Solar with the word *taitai,* a well-known peruanismo for father (p. 148). Instead of being presented as an example of the egregious abuses characteristic of the encomenderos and of the colony as a whole, the beating of the Indians is presented in terms reminiscent of the corporal punishment of children, an act until recently deemed socially acceptable due to its supposed pedagogic function.

This characterization of Indians as childlike posed an important problem for the construction of a national space. The idea of nationhood was based precisely on a theoretical equality among its members, since nationality supposedly overrode or rendered irrelevant any other characteristic that did not pertain to the nation. This national equality did not imply that there were no inequalities among the members of a nation; after all, poverty and exploitation were far from eradicated by the nationalist theories of the nineteenth century. Somewhat tautologically, what this notion of national equality meant was that only those differences that were related to the nation had any meaning for nationalistic thinking. Thus, depending on the conceptualization of the nation that was proposed, race, culture, or language would become the privileged criterion on which this equality was based. And, in fact, nationalism was in principle opposed to establishing any conceptual hierarchy among groups that were classified as belonging to the nation. (Slavery could be justified as long as the racial and ethnic groups in question were seen as external to the nation.) Thus, by classifying the Indians as childlike—that is, as individuals not qualified to participate in the national space—and by presenting them as adhering to specific cultural values alien to the "national" culture, "Carta canta" excludes the Amerindians from the nation.

"Carta canta" is, therefore, susceptible to mutually exclusive readings. If in one reading the Amerindians are the originators of national difference, in the other they are excluded from the nation. Paradoxically, "Carta canta" grounds the nation in that which it also excludes from the national space. The Indian, as the source of difference from Spain and the starting point of national history, is the privileged origin of the nation, but at the same time is situated by this text in a hierarchically inferior position to the Spanish conquerors, who are in turn represented as brutal interlopers in the nation and, simultaneously, described by the narrator as "our grandparents" (p. 147). In Palma's text, then, the country is shown to have a double origin. The conquistadors and the Indians are both sources of the nation: Spaniards as its genealogical origin ("our grandparents"), and the Indians as the historical and cultural origin of Peru's difference from other countries.

Palma's representation of the Indian as the origin of Peruvian difference is, however, complicated by the mediating role assigned to the Spanish conquerors. Not only is Solar the mediator between the Indian originators of "carta canta" and other Spanish speakers, but the narrator claims that it was in "reading the Jesuit Acosta" that he discovered the story he retells in the tradición (p. 147). Moreover, given that one can identify the narrator with the historical Palma, it is possible to extend the mediating role of the Spaniards from the tradición into the figure of the real-life Palma. Paradoxically, Palma's attempt in *Tradiciones peruanas* to achieve Peruvian and American cultural independence depends on the conquistadors' sketchy and biased representations of the conquest and of colonial society.

The contradictions in "Carta canta" are representative of those that will be found in later versions of the discourse of mestizaje. The tension between the rhetorical use of the Indian—or black—as the origin of national difference and the role played by mestizaje as a national ideology of nations governed by criollos is a constant in the texts I examine. But this contradiction is not limited to Spanish America; it is also the constitutive feature of Brazilian versions of the discourse of mestizaje and, in particular, of José de Alencar's Indianist novels.

CHAPTER FOUR

José de Alencar's Iracema

Mestizaje and the Fictional Foundation of Brazil

How can a new nation imagine an identity for itself independent from the metropolis with which it has identified, perhaps for centuries? How can populations that descend linguistically and culturally, if not racially, from European colonizers avoid establishing an identity that is not merely epigonic with respect to the former metropolis? How can a history of subordination to the metropolis become the basis for a new, independent cultural identity? These questions, which were central to Ricardo Palma's writing of *Tradiciones peruanas,* were also in the forefront of the intellectual production in Brazil, the other major cultural and linguistic area of South America. In fact, the search for an independent identity was, if anything, faced in a much more explicit manner in Brazil than in Spanish America. For instance, in 1840, under the auspices of the young Emperor Pedro II, the Instituto Histórico e Geográfico Brasileiro held a contest on how the history of Brazil should be written, which formed part of the country's search for an elusive national identity.

This preoccupation with defining Brazilian nationality will become manifest a few years later in the novels and plays of José de Alencar (1829–1877). In fact, Alencar's preoccupation with the role played by literature in the development of an independent national identity has led some critics to assign him a canonical position in the development of Brazilian literature. As Luis Fernando Valente (1994, 64) notes: "Alencar holds a position in the field of Brazilian literature similar to that of a Balzac in French literature, of a Shakespeare in English literature, of a Dante in Italian literature, of a Camões in Portuguese literature, and of a Cervantes in

Spanish literature, writers whose works represent watersheds in their respective literary traditions."

However, the first major theorization of Brazilian national identity was formulated not by Alencar nor by any other Brazilian intellectual, but curiously, by a foreigner, German botanist Karl Friedrich Phillipp von Martius, the winner of the contest sponsored by the Instituto Histórico e Geográfico. Martius wrote an essay claiming that the uniqueness of Brazil consisted in the presence and mixture of three cultural traditions and peoples: Portuguese, Indian, and African.[1] Martius's essay foreshadowed the most influential answer to the problems of identity in Brazil: the notion of a racial democracy in which the three foundational groups—originating in Europe, America, and Africa—were seen as contributors to the establishment of a new Brazilian culture and race.

The works of José de Alencar followed in the theoretical footsteps of Martius by postulating miscegenation and cultural interaction as the basis of Brazilian national identity. But, unlike the German scholar, Alencar did not take the African contribution into account, a glaring omission given the makeup of Brazil's population.[2] His concern with creating a literature representative of the nation as a whole led him, like his contemporary Palma, to cover much of the history and geography of the country in his writings. However, it is principally in his so-called "Indianist" novels—*O Guarani* (1857), *Ubirajara* (1874), and especially *Iracema* (1865)—that Alencar most fully fictionalized the problem of establishing a national identity independent and different from that of Portugal.

Iracema *as a Fictionalization of Nation Building*

Of these three novels, critical and popular opinion has singled out *Iracema* as Alencar's most successful fictionalization of the origin of the Brazilian nation.[3] Its story of a love affair between Iracema, an Indian priestess, and Martim, a Portuguese soldier, is more than a tragic story of forbidden love between the races. *Iracema* is the most complete nineteenth-century literary version of the archetypal story of the discourse of mestizaje—the union of the European man and the Amerindian woman from which a new race and nation are created.

Iracema can be read as providing a story of the origin of Brazil that sees the country as more than a continuation of Portugal. The central role assigned to the character of Iracema in this foundational narrative—the text, after all, is named after her—serves to emphasize the difference between Brazil and Portugal that is thematized in Alencar's novel. Although the original Brazilian edition of the novel is subtitled a *lenda* (legend), Alencar's narrative is characterized by a subtle manipulation of the boundaries between fiction and historical fact.[4] For instance, the foundation of the state of Ceará, a historical event, becomes the conclusion of Alencar's narrative,[5] and two of the main characters in the novel—Martim and Poti—are identified with the historical Martim Moreno and Poti (Antônio Felipe Camarão), two of the key players in the Portuguese opposition to the establishment of a Dutch colony in the seventeenth century. Moreover, Alencar substantiates every single innovation in style or story with numerous linguistic footnotes and a lengthy footnote entitled "Historical Argument." This parallel text—containing etymologies of geographical names, translations of Amerindian names, and the historical basis for the plot—creates a proliferation of factual details that attempts to establish the fictional elements of *Iracema* as compatible with history.

Iracema complicates the archetypal story of the discourse of *mestizaje* by placing Iracema's and Martim's love affair within the turmoil of northeastern Brazil in the early seventeenth century. This epoch is portrayed by Alencar as a period of internecine warfare among the Tupi Indians. This interethnic violence originates in the opposition between the rival French or Portuguese colonizers with whom each Tupi group is allied. Iracema, the daughter of a Tabajara priest, assists him preparing the hallucinatory *jurema* potion that, according to the novel, forms a central part of Tupi religious rituals. As part of her religious obligations, Iracema is expected to remain celibate. She, however, feels an intense attraction toward Martim and seduces him when he is under the spell of jurema.[6] Since the Tabajaras are allied with the French, in her romance with the Portuguese Martim she not only violates religious taboos but also rejects political alliances. Given the transgressive nature of their relationship, the lovers escape from the highlands where the Tabajara live to the coastal areas under the control of the Pitiguaras, who have sided with the Portuguese. At first, Iracema and Martim are content with their life together, but after seeing a French ship, which he mistakes for a Portuguese vessel, Martim becomes nostalgic for his homeland. Later, when his Pitiguara friend Poti informs him that the ship brought supplies and French soldiers, Martim decides to resume fighting. Not even Iracema's pregnancy keeps him at her side. Depressed and alone, she gives birth to Moacir, whom she calls "the child born of my suffering" (Alencar 2000, 101), and dies just after Martim's return. Martim leaves with the infant Moacir for Portugal. At the novel's end, however, he returns to the area where he once lived with Iracema and founds the city of Ceará. Poti joins his friend, converts to Catholicism, and vows fidelity to the Portuguese crown.

This fictionalization of the archetypal story of the discourse of mestizaje can be interpreted as privileging the Portuguese elements in the country's formation. The death of Iracema and Poti's embrace of a Portuguese identity in politics and religion can be read as implying the elimination of cultural diversity in Alencar's fictional foundation of Brazil. Moacir, the original Brazilian mestizo, is described by the narrator as "the first child that the blood of the white race had begotten in this land of freedom" (p. 100), thereby emphasizing the white filiation of the child. Moreover, Moacir is raised exclusively by his Portuguese father.[7] The Indian past is thus demoted to Brazil's prehistory while the fictional Brazil founded by Martim, although racially inclusive as evidenced by Poti's incorporation into the new colony, is culturally Portuguese.

However, a closer examination of the novel reveals that its representation of mestizaje as the origin of the Brazilian nation is more ambivalent than the previous analysis suggests. In fact, Iracema hesitates between privileging the Amerindian or Portuguese poles of the story and, within its narrative gaps, it denudes some of the contradictions at the heart of Brazilian versions of the discourse of mestizaje. The text may be viewed as consisting of two halves.[8] Iracema dominates the first part of the novel from their first meeting until Martim resumes fighting the French-Tabajara alliance. In this section, beginning with their meeting when she shoots an arrow at Martim, through their first sexual act, when she takes advantage of Martim's jurema-induced hallucination to seduce him, Iracema initiates and controls their relationship. The sexual freedom and agency accorded to Iracema as a character clearly contradict the image of women in nineteenth-century literature as sexually and socially subordinate to men.[9] Moreover, given the stress placed in the narrative on the racial identities of the main characters, the inversion of the traditional hierarchical relationship between men and women can be interpreted as a parallel modification of racial hierarchies. This inversion is explicitly thematized in the passage where Martim decides to become Tupi, a decision that is presented as a change of allegiance from Portugal to indigenous

Brazil: "The White Warrior desires no other homeland but that of his son and of his heart" (p. 79).

In order to be accepted as a Tupi, Martim participates in an initiation ceremony in which, after the colors of the tribe are painted on the prospective member, the warriors "wrote" on the initiate's skin: "They would vary the colors, and many warriors customarily wrote the symbols of their deeds" (p. 81). As befits Iracema's active role in the first part of the novel, she also participates in this ceremony: "Iracema took the vane of the feather and painted a bee on a tree leaf" (p. 82). The ceremony concludes with Iracema giving Martim a Tupi name: Cotiabo—"the painted warrior" (p. 82). Here the novel has virtually reversed the traditional pattern of assimilation at the heart of the discourse of mestizaje. Rather than the Amerindian being assimilated into Luso-Brazilian culture, it is the European colonizer who is incorporated into that of the Tupis; rather than giving a European name to the indigenous elements, it is the European who is newly baptized. Redefining his identity, Martim abandons his European past for an Amerindian present. He even changes his name and declares loyalty to "Indo-Brazil." Moreover, the ceremony underscores the emphasis on Amerindian agency typical of the first half of the novel: Martin is completely passive while Iracema and Poti "write" on his body. In fact, if we accept René Jara's and Nicholas Spadaccini's association of inscription with penetration and of the writing surface with the female Indian body, it could be argued that this ceremony implies a complete reversal of the male and female, as well as European and Indian, roles and agency characteristic of the conquest of America (Jara and Spadaccini 1992).

Yet, precisely at the moment when *Iracema* threatens to subvert the Eurocentric and patriarchal basis of Brazilian identity by extolling the superiority and seductiveness of Amerindian culture, the narrative takes a turn that restores traditional hierarchical relations between Tupi and Portuguese, as well as between man and woman. This second section of the novel begins when Martim sees a ship in the distance: "The Christian knew it was a large boat with many sails, such as his brothers built; and longing for his homeland gripped his heart" (Alencar 2000, 85). Predictably, Martim's remembrance of his European and Portuguese identity is linked to his assumption of an active role in his relationship with Iracema, who is now relegated to a subordinate position. Iracema's handing over of

Moacir and her subsequent death can be interpreted as the logical conclusion of her gradual loss of agency and power in the narrative. As Ria Lemaire (1989, 63) puts it, "Thus, reduced to passivity (to waiting) and to muteness, i.e., put to death mentally and culturally, Iracema has to die physically as well."

When Martim returns to Ceará at the end of the novel, his brief adoption of a Tupi identity as Cotiabo is completely forgotten. He establishes a Portuguese settlement and brings with him a Catholic priest. The ending is particularly significant in that it is, in fact, nothing less than the reversal of the Tupi initiation ceremony. Whereas in the first ceremony Martim changes his name and becomes Tupi—even if only temporarily—the ending has Poti converting to Catholicism and changing his name forever: "Poti was the first who knelt at the foot of the sacred wood. . . . As his baptismal name he received that of the saint whose day it was, and that of the king whom he was to serve, followed by his own, in the language of his new brothers" (p. 112). Poti, who is a chief of the Pitiguaras and repeatedly describes himself Martim's brother (e.g., pp. 40, 46, 54, 59, 87), becomes a subject of the Portuguese king and a member of the Catholic Church. However, in a utopian gesture, the text describes Poti's position in the new Luso-Brazil as that of an equal with the Portuguese settlers: he is still described as a brother (p. 112). Moreover, as Alencar notes in the "Historical Argument," Poti is better known as Felipe Camarão, "a name he glorified in the war against the Dutch" (p. 116).

But in spite of this apparently egalitarian description of Poti's role in Brazilian history, it is necessary to underscore that he has to give up his identity as a Pitiguara—including his religion, culture, and political power—and assume the position and culture of a Portuguese subject in order to assimilate into the newly founded Brazil and become one of its first heroes. In fact, Poti's assimilation seems to imply not only a complete abandonment of his indigenous past, but even active opposition to it. The novel notes somewhat laconically that "some time later, when Albuquerque, the great leader of the white warriors, came, Martim and Camarão departed for the banks of the Mearim to wreak punishment upon the fierce Tupinambás and expel the white barbarian enemy" (p. 112). Poti goes from being a Tupi chief, to being an active enemy of his former culture and people. The novel goes from sympathetically describing indigenous peoples and traditions to classifying them, together with non-Portuguese/Brazilian whites, as outside not only the field of Brazilian nationality but even of civilization. (The Tupi are described as fierce, while non-Portuguese Europeans are classified as barbarians.)

Iracema, therefore, implicitly accepts Amerindians into its fictionalization of the nation, but only if they exchange their Indian identity for a Luso-Brazilian one. But this Luso-Brazilian identity has among its requirements both political yielding and religious submission—Poti vows to serve the Portuguese king and kneels before the cross. Unlike the horizontal and egalitarian relationships characteristic of the Tupi tribes, and of Martim's relationship with the Indians, the newly founded Brazil is shown to be both egalitarian (as implied in the "brotherhood" of the members of the nation) and, paradoxically, hierarchical (as exemplified in the establishment of religious and political institutions based on the subordination of its members). Moreover, unassimilated Indians, such as Iracema or the "fierce Tupinambá," whom the novel fully identifies with Indo-Brazil, are tellingly kept outside the new country.

The foundation of the Brazilian nation is, therefore, predicated on the establishment of the conventional relations between the sexes and races, which had been subverted in the first half of *Iracema.* Claims to hegemonic completion are, however, undermined by the nostalgia that informs the novel. The text begins with Martim's tearful gaze at the land where Iracema's grave lies, and it ends with Martim walking on the same land, which is now under Portuguese control, "the bitter longing in his breast" (p. 112).

This nostalgic tone, which in a first reading may seem disconcerting in "the Brazilian national epic" (Schwamborn 1990, 191), can be interpreted as the trace of the historical reality on which Brazil is constructed: the genocide of the Brazilian Indian. Instead of experiencing a "gentle" death like Iracema, the great majority of Indians were killed or brutally overworked by the Portuguese colonizers and their descendants. If death was often the price of assimilation, punishment or, better said, massacre, was that of resistance. As was often the case throughout the Americas, the usurpation of Indian land and the exploitation of their labor became the basis for Brazilian colonial prosperity until indigenous population decline forced the Portuguese to import Africans as an alternative slave labor force. *Iracema,* however, transmutes this foundational historical genocide into the tragic story of a woman dying for love, into a story of nostalgia— "the bitter longing"—and into the name Moacir—"child born of suffering." Iracema's death, and the sense of loss it infuses into the narrative, thus becomes both a sign of the genocide that is never mentioned in the novel and an example of how Alencar attempts to eliminate the historical conflict between the Portuguese and Indians in his fiction. Even the Tupinambá allied with the "foreign barbarians" are described as being only "punished," not exterminated or enslaved.

Critics have read the elimination of historical conflict in *Iracema* as part of the creation of a myth narrating the origin of Brazilian nationality.[10] It is precisely the substitution of a "timeless" love story for the brutal historical fact of the genocide of the Amerindian that not only makes *Iracema*'s national myth palatable to large sectors of the country's multiethnic population but also allows the novel to function as an agent of cohesion in the construction of Brazilian nationality.

The Tension between Edenic Myth and Historical Reality

There is in *Iracema,* as a national text, a tension between its mythic value and the historical reality that is being fictionalized. If the novel imagines a national origin acceptable to all readers, it must also ensure that this origin is—at least superficially—compatible with historical facts. This tension becomes visible in Alencar's apparent need to buttress this love story set in a quasi-Edenic space with historical and factual footnotes and with the "Historical Argument."

A particularly significant moment of such tension between the historical and factual narrative in the footnotes and the mythical story in the text is in the passage in which Martim and Poti visit Maranguab, Poti's grandfather (Alencar 2000, 74–76). Maranguab, once the greatest of all Pitiguara warriors, is at the time of their visit old and living alone far from the rest of his tribe. In the passage where he receives Martim and Poti, Maranguab declares, "Tupã has willed that before losing their sight these eyes should see the white hawk beside the *narceja* [a kind of snipe]" (p. 75). Although Maranguab's statement seems to present a figure of harmony in which the European white hawk peacefully stands beside the Brazilian narceja, Alencar inserts a footnote that emphasizes the contradiction, even violence, hidden in the image. There, Alencar explains Maranguab's juxtaposition of the snipe and the hawk as a prophecy of "the destruction of his race by the white race" (p. 127). The historical extermination of the Amerindians at the hands of the Europeans is thus introduced into a novel whose narrative attempts to eliminate, or at least minimize, the violence between these two groups. But the mention of the genocide of the Brazilian Indian is displaced outside the body of the narrative text into Alencar's historical and linguistic footnotes. Moreover, in a second (temporal) displacement, the genocide of the Indian is presented as a prophecy to be fulfilled beyond the time frame of the narrative.

The tension between myth and history can also be seen in the development of the story line, which begins, as we have seen, in a prehistorical—or perhaps ahistorical—Eden where Indians and whites live, if not in perfect harmony (since the Pitiguara battle the Tabajara), at least in a world devoid of hierarchies. The Portuguese Martim is constantly described as a brother, that is, as neither superior nor inferior to his Pitiguara allies. The novel concludes, however, in a historical world where hierarchical differentiation between the Amerindian and the Portuguese has been established, since it is the cultural values of the latter group that exclusively define national identity.[11] Therefore, unlike Martim's voluntary Tupi conversion, Poti's incorporation into the Portuguese colony implies not only a shift in his allegiance and culture, but the acceptance of a rigid hierarchical religious and social organization. The text's nostalgic tone is itself testimony to the sense of loss caused not only by the genocide of the Indian but by the passing of this Edenic state, an occurrence that is itself the necessary condition for the founding of Brazil. *Iracema* is a foundational myth in which the foundation of Brazil is also seen as implying a profound and much-lamented loss. Brazil is founded, but the price paid is the disappearance of its aboriginal cultures and the egalitarian way of life that is their central characteristic. It is this loss, not only the fictional Iracema's painful and solitary experience of giving birth, that explains why the first Brazilian is called "child of suffering." Moacir is the product of a genocide and destruction that leave a void for which not even the (partial) genetic survival of the Indian in miscegenation can fully compensate.

The elimination, or at least understatement, of the central historical conflict between Indians and Portuguese is typical of Alencar's Indianist novels as a group. In fact, if one looks at these novels chronologically, the conflict between the Portuguese and the Indians is progressively eliminated from Alencar's representations of the founding of Brazil. In *O Guarani* (1857), the story of the Guarani chief Peri's platonic love for the Portuguese woman Cecilia Mariz is framed by the story of the armed struggle between the noble Portuguese Mariz family and the Aimorés, an

Indian tribe that, unlike the Guarani, are described in subhuman terms. In *Iracema* (1865), as we have seen, the only explicit violence presented is between Indians, and the genocide of the Amerindians is transmuted into the tragic story of Iracema's ill-fated love. In fact, the elimination of historical contradictions from Alencar's novels reaches its logical conclusion in his final Indianist novel, *Ubirajara* (1874), in which the Portuguese are excluded altogether from the foundational story. In *Ubirajara,* Alencar presents a narrative of mestizaje that occurs exclusively among Amerindian tribes. This novel displaces the Portuguese to the role of yet another tribe, the future Caramurus, who will in turn be assimilated into a Brazil characterized by a process of biological and cultural mixture that includes but also predates the Portuguese presence (Alencar [1874] 1977, 144). It is only in the footnotes, which (as in *Iracema*) Alencar uses to supplement the narrative with historical and linguistic information, that the Portuguese presence is discussed. Of course, although in *Ubirajara* Alencar successfully eliminates the violence of the conquest, he no longer provides a verisimilar foundational narrative for a Brazilian society clearly defined by Portuguese colonization.

Brazilian versus Spanish American Versions of Mestizaje

The presentation of Brazil as founded through a nonviolent conquest marks a central difference between Brazilian versions of the discourse of mestizaje and Spanish American ones.[12] While in some of *Ubirajara*'s historical footnotes Alencar criticizes the treatment of the Indians by the Portuguese,[13] the bulk of his writings, as well as the ideological position he takes in them, present the conquest as a moment of positive cultural and sexual encounter rather than as a period of conflict and extermination, even if it is possible to find traces of the genocide of the Brazilian Indians in them. This take on the historical conflict between the Indians and the Portuguese is characteristic of the Brazilian discourse of mestizaje. Later theorists of the nation such as Gilberto Freyre, in *Casa-Grande e Senzala* (1933), and Sérgio Buarque de Holanda, in *Raízes do Brasil* (1936)—present the colonization of Brazil as based on the harmonious collaboration among Portuguese, Amerindians, and Afro-Brazilians.

One possible explanation for this difference between Spanish American and Brazilian versions of the discourse of mestizaje in terms of the representation of Indian and European conflict may be found in the relations of these two cultural areas with their metropolises. Spanish America achieved independence only after a bloody and protracted struggle that lasted for fourteen years, beginning with the first independence governments in 1810 (Bushnell and Macaulay 1994, 18). Brazilian independence, on the other hand, lacked a significant military struggle against the former metropolis. In fact, Brazilian independence is arguably defined by a sense of continuity with the colonial past. Not only was the first emperor, Pedro I, the son of the Portuguese monarch, but in 1831 he succeeded to the European throne after having ruled Brazil for nine years. Alencar's nonrepresentation of violence between his Amerindian and Portuguese protagonists thus parallels the absence of a significant historical enmity between the Brazilian and Portuguese elites. While the Spanish American criollos also had close ties with Spain, they were also the inheritors of a history of antagonism between the colony and the metropolis. As we have seen, the condemnation of the conquest, so ingrained in, for instance, Ricardo Palma's writings, implies an attempt to differentiate criollos from Spaniards and to hide the obvious links between the two groups. Alencar's and most Brazilian versions of the discourse of mestizaje do not deny the links between the Brazilian elites and their Portuguese ancestors, but on the contrary try to minimize the foundational violence of the extermination of the Indian and the later exploitation of blacks from their version of history. While the discourse of mestizaje became in both cultural areas the ideological basis of the nation, the discrepancies between the versions proposed reflect the particular histories of Spanish America and Brazil.

Alencar's version of the discourse of mestizaje, however, has in common with Spanish American ones the representation of the Indian as the source of national difference. Alencar, like many Spanish American authors, presents the Amerindian as the principal, if not the exclusive, source of biological and cultural difference from Europe. His hesitations between privileging indigenous or Portuguese elements in *Iracema* exemplifies his attempt at simultaneously emphasizing Brazilian difference from Portugal and the cultural and racial continuity between both nations.

Later Brazilian theorists of the nation will attempt to resolve Alencar's contradictions (as would Alencar himself in his final narrative of national origins, *Ubirajara,* which as we have seen, excludes the European elements from his allegorical version of Brazil). However, while later writers will continue Alencar's stress on the heterogeneous origin of the nation, the de-emphasis, even the practical elimination, of the Amerindian as a formative element becomes the solution to the contradiction between the Tupi and Portuguese elements in their conceptualization of the nation. As we shall see, Gilberto Freyre, perhaps the most influential national theorist in twentieth-century Brazil, proposes a version of a nation that, while accepting Amerindian and especially black cultural elements, still celebrates the Portuguese as the formative element of the nation.

Yet Alencar's Indianist novels have also given rise to a more literary and less politically conservative progeny. For instance, it is widely acknowledged that the reworking of the figure of the Indian as representative of Brazilian identity to be found in texts such as Mário de Andrade's *Macunaíma* (1928) and Oswald de Andrade's "Manifesto antropófago" (1928) imply both a continuation—even in the case of Oswald de Andrade, who lampoons Alencar—and a radicalization of Alencar's work (see Valente 1994, 142–43, 146–47).

It is possible, therefore, to identify Alencar as one of the sources of twentieth-century redefinitions of identity developed by authors as diverse and as influential as Freyre, Buarque de Holanda, Oswald, and Mário. This influence makes Alencar's Indianist novels still a significant starting point for any reflection on Brazilian thinking about national difference. But, paradoxically, Alencar's continuing relevance is rooted in his contradictions, in his hesitation between privileging the Tupi or the Portuguese as the source of Brazilian nationality.

CHAPTER FIVE

Gilberto Freyre's
Casa-Grande e Senzala

Mestizaje as a Family Affair

Ever since its publication in 1933, Gilberto Freyre's historico-anthropological study *Casa-Grande e Senzala* has occupied a central position in the Brazilian imagination.[1] At the core of this text's appeal is the fact that, unlike earlier commentators, Freyre presented an optimistic vision of Brazilian society and its history. This optimism was based in Freyre's anti-racialist stance, which rightfully has been seen as a revolutionary departure from the monotonous and pessimistic repetitions of pseudoscientific platitudes about inferior races and the degenerative effects of miscegenation characteristic of most previous writings about the country. Moreover, the influence of *Casa-Grande e Senzala* quickly went beyond the sphere of the social sciences, and its basic premises soon became points of departure for the work of numerous authors and artists from Freyre's time on. The statements of intellectuals and artists as diverse as novelist Jorge Amado, literary critic Antônio Candido, anthropologist Darcy Ribeiro, and filmmaker Nelson Pereira dos Santos exemplify Freyre's widespread and lasting mark on Brazilian culture.[2] Freyre's influence has even reached Brazil's general population. One of the highlights of the 1962 carnival in Rio de Janeiro was the presentation by the popular "samba school" Mangueira of a pageant inspired by *Casa-Grande e Senzala* (Freyre [1933] 1995, xxviii).

The emphasis in *Casa-Grande e Senzala* on the contribution of Afro-

Brazilians to the formation of a national identity lies at the center of Freyre's continuing influence. Unlike José de Alencar, who described a Brazil founded by love affairs between Portuguese and Indians and peopled by those two groups and their descendants, Freyre also recognized the contribution of Brazilian blacks to the national culture. This new stress on the participation of blacks in Brazilian history and culture corresponds much more closely than did Alencar's Indianism to the makeup of the Brazilian population. For instance, according to the census figures of 1940, seven years after the publication of *Casa-Grande e Senzala,* 40 percent of the population claimed to be of African descent (Skidmore 1974, 45). This figure may in fact underrepresent the black and mulatto population of Brazil. In Latin America the racial classifications in census figures are considered unreliable. In Brazil, as in most of Latin America, individuals who are perceived to be white—regardless of their actual family background—have a social and economic advantage. Moreover, race is only one of the criteria by which whiteness is defined. Economic position and education are other significant attributes associated with racial classifications (see Skidmore 1974, 39–44; Stam 1997, 45–46). Therefore, Freyre's emphasis on the importance of the cultural contributions of Afro-Brazilians had "a revolutionary impact" on Brazilian readers who until then had been accustomed to texts that, at best, denied the importance of the country's large black and mulatto population (Candido [1967] 1995, 10).

But the question remains why blacks, despite their numerical significance and concomitant cultural influence, had been ignored in discourse about the nation. Alencar's works may serve as a starting point to answer this question. Alencar's exclusion of blacks from his representation of Brazil has been explained either by referring to his own politically conservative and pro-slavery position or through allegorical readings of his novels in which the Amerindian characters are read as representing black slaves.[3] While there are elements of truth in both explanations, these readings of Alencar's novels do not take into account the ideological values associated with the different racial groups in nineteenth-century Brazil. Alencar's emphasis on the Tupi, and his concomitant marginalization of blacks, might also be read as part of an attempt—however contradictory—to establish a sense of national specificity grounded in a source both independent from Portugal and native to America.

Unlike Amerindians, blacks were frequently seen as indissolubly linked to the Portuguese who brought them to Brazil as slaves. Furthermore, it was common for slave owners and their intellectual allies to claim as part of their ideological justification for slavery that blacks were servile by nature.[4] This characterization of blacks as submissive was not influenced even by the proliferation of *quilombos* (settlements of escaped slaves) or the heroic resistance to the colonial armies by the largest of these, Palmares, during much of the seventeenth century.[5] Furthermore, by Alencar's time, as "cultural others" the Indians were conveniently distant from Brazilian urban centers and thus easily celebrated by writers who did not have to consider the exploitation of indigenous groups. Blacks, however, were the daily companions of the Portuguese, and later Brazilian, elites. They were the elites' cooks, nannies, servants, and according to Freyre and other Brazilian writers, their sexual partners. Moreover, this exclusion of blacks from writings about the nation was reinforced by the practical emphasis placed by scientific racialism and its popularizers on the absolute inferiority of blacks.

By the first decades of the twentieth century, however, the dogmas of racialism had begun to be challenged and contradicted by scientists and intellectuals in the Americas and in Europe. An intellectual climate was therefore created in Brazil in which not only could the discourse of mestizaje become the dominant ideological basis for a new theorization of nationality, but the conceptual incorporation of blacks into the nation could be contemplated. Moreover, because slaves in Brazil had been liberated in 1888, there were no longer any economic interests opposing the inclusion of blacks into historical, theoretical, or fictional representations of the nation. It is in this new ideological climate that Gilberto Freyre—a former student of Franz Boas, one of the principal debunkers of racialism in the United States—was able to propose a new version of the discourse of mestizaje that not only included blacks but also seemed to privilege their role in the foundation of nationality.

In *Casa-Grande e Senzala* (1933), Freyre presents a historical vision of Brazil in which Portuguese, Indians, and blacks are contributors—though not necessarily in equal degrees—to the formation of a national ethos. The starting point for Freyre's version of the historical formation of Brazil is the fact that there were few women among the Portuguese who colonized the country. Therefore, the Portuguese conquerors and colonizers had to take Indian or black women as sexual partners, lovers, and eventually wives. According to Freyre, the consequence of this social and sexual intercourse among Portuguese men and Indian and black women was that the relationship between hegemonic and subaltern groups was "mitigated by the need that was felt by many colonists of founding a family under such circumstances and upon such a basis as this" (Freyre 1956, xxix). For Freyre, it was "the lubricating oil of deep-going miscegenation" that helped ease the social tensions among the three racial groups present during the Portuguese colonization of Brazil (p. 182).

Even though the relationship between these three founding groups was based on the exploitation by the Portuguese of the conquered Indians and enslaved blacks, Freyre believes that miscegenation between Portuguese men and Indian and black women had a profoundly egalitarian effect: "Hybrid from the beginning, Brazilian society is, of all those in the Americas, the one most harmoniously constituted so far as racial relations are concerned, within the environment of a practical cultural reciprocity that results in the advanced people deriving the maximum of profit from the values and experiences of the backward ones, and in a maximum of conformity between the foreign and the native cultures, that of the conqueror and that of the conquered" (p. 83). According to Freyre, it was the presence of Indian and later black women within Portuguese households that ensured the incorporation of indigenous and African customs and cultural products into Brazilian colonial society. Since Africans and Indians were adapted to the tropics, the incorporation of these customs and products favored the development of a new Portuguese-based culture suited to the South American environment. Moreover, this contact between Portuguese, Indians, and blacks ultimately led to the formation of a national culture that was common to all three groups regardless of their position in the social structure.

But the subversion of cultural hierarchies was not the only consequence of miscegenation. Even economic and social divisions are described by Freyre as being eased by the "lubricating oil" of sexual interaction. A plantation economy, such as that of colonial and imperial Brazil, implies the oppression of a large number of black slaves by a small aristocracy of white landowners and the near-elimination of an intermediate class of free farmers or artisans. Miscegenation, however, is described by Freyre as creating a racially mixed intermediate group that acted both as a buffer between the two opposing social groups and, by creating cultural bonds between them, as an agent of cultural change for progressively more egalitarian relations among them. Thus, for Freyre the social polarization of plantation owners and oppressed slaves "was in good part offset by the social effects of miscegenation. The Indian woman and the 'mina,' or Negro woman, in the beginning, and later the mulatto, the *cabrocha,* the quadroon, and the octoroon, becoming domestics, concubines, and even the lawful wives of their white masters, exerted a powerful influence for social democracy in Brazil" (p. xxx).

Miscegenation is also seen as an influence in the development of egalitarian patterns of landownership in Brazil. According to Freyre, by willing land to their numerous mulatto sons—both legitimate and illegitimate—the landowners unwittingly promoted the progressive partition of the plantations (p. l). Thus, miscegenation, in this analysis, also became an egalitarian and democratic influence in the economic formation of Brazil.

Despite Freyre's frequent emphasis on the importance of the distinction between race and culture, which he learned from Boas,[6] his analysis depends on a conception of both cultural and biological mestizaje. In fact, both culture and race ultimately become identified with each other, since it is the miscegenation between biologically diverse white, black, and indigenous groups that is seen as the source of the parallel cultural fusion. Freyre's dependence on the concept of race is manifested in his belief that races have hereditary biological and psychological adaptations to their environment (pp. 285–89). Thus, in his analysis, the explanation for the adaptation to the tropical environment of Brazil by the mestizo, mulatto, and nominally white but actually racially mixed populations originated in the miscegenation of the Portuguese with the Indians and blacks (p. 13).

While his emphasis on race is another example of the slippage between race and culture that is characteristic of much writing about mestizaje, Freyre's use of racial classifications often leads him to reintroduce racial hierarchies that supposedly have been eliminated from his analysis. For example, in *Casa-Grande e Senzala* he states that the cultural superiority of the slaves brought to Brazil implies that "Brazil benefited from a better type of colonist from the 'dark continent' than did other countries of America, the United States for example" (p. 306). Freyre explicitly establishes a hierarchical classification of the African population in which some groups are seen as "better" or superior to others.

Equally symptomatic of Freyre's inability to fully renounce racialist hierarchies and concepts are the anti-Semitic statements scattered throughout *Casa-Grande e Senzala.* The following quotation can serve as an example of this strain present in his writings: "The Jews became technicians in usury, thanks to a quasi-biological process of specialization that seems to have sharpened their faces to resemble that of a bird of prey, their gestures mimicking those of acquisition and taking possession, their hands becoming claws incapable of sowing or creating. Their hands are capable only of hoarding" (Freyre [1933] 1995, 226; my translation).[7] In spite of the qualification "quasi," which permits Freyre to affirm the existence of a process of biological specialization while simultaneously denying scientific validity to the phenomenon just described, it is difficult not to align the preceding passage with the worst stereotypes of racialism. By associating Jews exclusively with money lending and by describing them in animalistic terms, Freyre echoes contemporary European anti-Semitic discourse. (*Casa-Grande e Senzala* was published in 1933, the same year Hitler came to power.) Although both Freyre's hierarchization of the African population and his anti-Semitism are tangential to his basic argument that claims to celebrate black contributions to Brazil, his occasional racialism is symptomatic of the limits of his egalitarian position.

Freyre implicitly establishes a similar hierarchization of the different races that make up the Brazilian population. He considers Indians to be inferior physically and culturally to Africans (Freyre 1956, 284–90), and their contribution less significant than that of the Africans or the Portuguese in the formation of the nation.[8] In a passage quoted previously, Freyre provides a brief history of mestizaje in which the Indian woman is present only in the first moment of colonization and is almost immediately replaced by the African woman and her descendants: "The Indian woman and the 'mina,' or Negro woman, in the beginning" (p. xxx). *Casa-Grande e Senzala* privileges the role of Afro-Brazilians over that of the Indians in the formation of a national identity and, therefore, provides an alternative foundational narrative to Alencar's narrative (which in other respects Freyre continues). Freyre's celebration of the black contribution to Brazilian society created a significant impetus for the study of Afro-Brazilian culture, as well as for the rise of a literature, such as that of Jorge Amado, centered on black characters and traditions.[9]

But despite its emphasis on the Afro-Brazilian contributions to Brazilian identity, *Casa-Grande e Senzala* presents a vision of history clearly compatible with the ideology of whitening. Freyre gives a summary of the history of miscegenation in which the "Negro woman" is succeeded by "the mulatto, the *cabrocha,* the quadroon, and the octoroon" (p. xxx), that is, by progressively whiter descendants of blacks. Therefore, *Casa-Grande e Senzala* arguably achieves the apparently impossible feat of being both a landmark in the acceptance and valorization of black Brazilians and also a more sophisticated version of whitening compatible, if not with racialism as a totalizing ideology, at least with many racist beliefs and assumptions.[10]

Despite the presence of racialism in Freyre's analysis of Brazilian history, *Casa-Grande e Senzala* gained acceptance as an egalitarian reconceptualization of Brazilian identity. Miscegenation became synonymous with a racial democracy that presented a historical version of Brazil formed by the contributions of its three constitutive races—Indian, black, and white—and, thus, implied the validation and acceptance of these originating racial and cultural groups (even if the Amerindian cultural contribution is undervalued by Freyre). Moreover, as we have seen, Freyre's conceptualization of Brazil was more concordant with the actual makeup of the population than were earlier works, such as those of Alencar.

This interpretation of *Casa-Grande e Senzala* as presenting an idyllic vision of racial relations in colonial Brazil has been prevalent even among Freyre's antagonists. Whether criticizing his work for its obfuscation of class differences or finding in *Casa-Grande e Senzala* a myth of racial harmony that serves to deny existing discrimination against blacks, most critics continue to read Freyre's study as a description of Brazil as a harmonious racial democracy.[11]

But if there is strong textual basis for seeing in *Casa-Grande e Senzala* an optimistic vision of Brazil and its history, there is also a solid basis for reading it as a chronicle of the violence and exploitation of slaves and Amerindians that characterized Brazil's colonial past and its plantation economy. In fact, Freyre is well aware that the wealth of the casa-grande originated "at the expense of slave labor" (p. 24), and that "the sweat and at times the blood of Negroes was the oil, rather than that of the whale, that helped to give the Big House foundations their fortress-like consistency" (p. xxxv). Moreover, *Casa-Grande e Senzala* gives numerous examples of the brutality with which plantation owners as a class frequently treated their slaves: female slaves forced into prostitution by their owners (p. 454), young slave boys physically and sexually abused by the pubescent sons of the plantation owners (p. 75), etc. And Freyre's description of the relationship between the Portuguese and the Indians shows a similar awareness of the violence that characterized both the conquest of the land

and the enslavement of its aboriginal inhabitants. Freyre points out the economic source of the extermination of the Indians through overwork in the sugar plantations: "It was sugar that killed the Indian" (p. 179).

Freyre even contradicts his central vision of miscegenation as a harmonious coupling of Portuguese men with Amerindian and black women by pointing out that the relationships described in *Casa-Grande e Senzala* did not originate in the union of equals, but rather were predicated on the power and control held by the Portuguese conquerors over their Indian subjects and African slaves: "The furious lust of the Portuguese men must have been exercised on victims who were not always partners in pleasure" (Freyre [1933] 1995, 50; my translation).[12] In fact, one cannot but come to the conclusion that the origin of the cultural and biological mestizaje so valued by Freyre depends on this inequality of power between Portuguese men and Indian or black women, rather than on the specious attribution of heightened sexual desire to Indian women and Portuguese men, which is also proposed in the text as an alternative explanation for miscegenation.[13] Moreover, even miscegenation, the central concept organizing Freyre's arguments and the basis for his optimistic evaluation of Brazilian history and society, is shown to have a profoundly negative aspect: a permanent and generalized epidemic of syphilis.

The importance of syphilis in Freyre's analysis has not been sufficiently emphasized.[14] In spite of his optimistic evaluation of the Brazilian population's adaptation to the country's tropical climate, there persists in Freyre's analysis a malaise about what he believes to be the genetic and physical deterioration and inferiority of this racially mixed people. In the introduction to the first edition, Freyre describes *Casa-Grande e Senzala* as originating in his own doubts about the human value of Brazil's racially mixed population: "And of all the problems confronting Brazil there was none that gave so much anxiety as that of miscegenation" (1956, xxvi). He even describes Brazilian mulattoes and mestizos as "caricatures of men" (p. xxvii). However, Freyre is able to propose a generalized epidemic of syphilis among the Brazilian population as the origin of and explanation for the supposed inferiority of Brazilians when compared to "unmixed" individuals (p. 47). Thus, he says, "The advantage of miscegenation in Brazil ran parallel to the tremendous disadvantage of syphilis. These two factors began operating at the same time: one to form the Brazilian, the ideal type of the tropics, a European with Negro or Indian blood to revive his energy; the other to deform him" (p. 71).

Syphilis is, paradoxically, the condition that makes it possible for Freyre to present his optimistic vision of miscegenation and mestizaje. Freyre's historical theory of a generalized and permanent epidemic of syphilis in Brazil enables him to deny the racialist dogma of the degeneration of the hybrid as an explanation for the supposed inferiority of the Brazilian population, which at some level he accepts. Therefore, syphilis and malnutrition allow Freyre to reject racialism, at least nominally.[15] His attribution of Brazilian physical degeneration to these causes makes it possible for him to be optimistic about the future of Brazil. Since both syphilis and malnutrition are treatable, this imagined Brazilian inferiority can be overcome by public health measures.

However, the presence of such profound contradictions in *Casa-Grande e Senzala* raises a series of questions regarding the interpretation of Freyre's text. For even if syphilis, malnutrition, and inequality are seen as the conditions that permit Freyre to valorize mestizaje and the contributions of blacks, Indians, mestizos, and mulattoes, must one conclude that disease, hunger, and injustice have a positive value? Moreover, while Freyre claims to find explanations of and even solutions for the presumed inferiority of the Brazilian population, the fact is that his analysis accepts this reputed racial inferiority as one of its starting points. Finally, one must also explain why it is that *Casa-Grande e Senzala,* in spite of its descriptions of the injustices of slavery, has generally been read as presenting an optimistic and harmonious vision of Brazilian history.

The Brazilian Population as a Colonial Family

Despite Freyre's awareness of the racial and class oppositions in Brazilian society, it is possible to interpret *Casa-Grande e Senzala* as a narrative of racial harmony because the contradictions in the text are domesticated, though not eliminated, by the central characteristic of Freyre's analysis of Brazilian history and society: the synecdochical reduction of the Brazilian population to the patriarchal colonial family. In other words, the "excess" generated by the text's numerous contradictions is contained by the fact that *Casa-Grande e Senzala* is, as its original subtitle indicates, a historical narrative of the "formation of the Brazilian family."[16] By presenting Brazilian history as a family saga, Freyre implicitly establishes limits for the racial and class tensions described in his text. In *Casa-Grande e Senzala,* class and racial strife become family squabbles.

While the title of *Casa-Grande e Senzala* implies the structural division of Brazilian society into two oppositional spaces and groups—the plantation house, populated by the elite white Portuguese family, and the slave quarters, where the oppressed Africans live—the text does not stress the racial and economic contradictions between the two spaces and groups. Instead, it places an almost exclusive emphasis on the casa-grande (plantation house), while mentioning the senzala (slave quarters) only sporadically. It is important to note, however, that the emphasis placed on the plantation house does not imply the exclusion of black Brazilians from Freyre's analysis. On the contrary, Freyre not only incorporates blacks, both slave and free, into the casa-grande, but also describes them as constitutive members of the patriarchal family. However, by systematically substituting the casa-grande for the senzala as the space in which the relationships among the different ethnic and social groups take place, he implicitly marginalizes the brutal exploitation of the field slaves, both male and female, who lived in the slave quarters.

Freyre's description of mestizaje, as previously noted, has as its foundational moment the sexual union of the Portuguese man and the Indian (later the black) woman. According to Freyre, it is precisely as sexual partners that Indian and especially black women are originally brought into the casa-grande. As he states, "the families in tropical Brazil that have remained white or almost white are few in number" (p. 267). Freyre's narrative continues the story of interracial romance found in Iracema, but in *Casa-Grande e Senzala,* the Indian (or black) woman survives and establishes a permanent relationship with the Portuguese man. However, the incorporation of the Indian or black woman into the foundational Brazilian family described by Freyre does not imply the elimination of slavery, since the patriarchal family is described as having a fundamentally different constitution from that of the modern nuclear family.

Because *Casa-Grande e Senzala* reads Brazilian history almost exclusively through the patriarchal family, the incorporation of the Indian and, principally, the black woman into Freyre's foundational Brazilian family has a number of important consequences. Since for Freyre, "the social history of the Big House is the intimate history of practically every Brazilian" (p. xliii), his analysis of the colonial family can be read as descriptive of the Brazilian nation as a whole. Given that the traditional family structure appears to be both a natural institution and one based on the existence of hierarchical relations among its members, the use of the family to represent Brazil implies the naturalization of social inequalities.[17] Moreover, by analyzing slavery within a domestic setting, rather than as an economic and social institution, *Casa-Grande e Senzala* transforms economic exploitation into a familial relationship. Thus, one of the consequences of the modular role assigned by Freyre to the patriarchal family is that the social dimension of the relationship between classes and races is transmuted into the psychological. The structural violence that had its origin in the economic exploitation that defines the relationship between master and slave is reduced in Freyre's analyses to emotional and psychological anomalies such as sadism (in the case of the Brazilian landowners) and masochism (in the case of the slaves).[18]

The representation of blacks and Indians as principally female sexual partners is another important consequence of Freyre's use of the family as a figure for the nation. By limiting the analysis of subaltern groups to the black or Indian woman, *Casa-grande e Senzala* mirrors one of the characteristic tropes of racialism that identified "savagery" with a "feminized state of childhood" and the "civilized" European with "full manly adulthood" (Young 1995, 94).[19] It is therefore not surprising that, apart from women, the only other nonwhite character incorporated into Freyre's narrative of the casa-grande is the whipping boy, the slave child who served as playmate for and victim of the plantation owner's child (p. 349).

Freyre acknowledges the role played by Indian women during the early colonial period, describing them as "the physical basis of the Brazilian family" (p. 87). He also claims that, as a consequence of their long interaction with the Moors, Portuguese men preferred "dark" women (pp. 11–13). Despite these statements, once Freyre begins an in-depth study of the colonial family, the mother and wife is always Portuguese. Indian women disappear from Freyre's narrative after the first period of colonization; black and mulatto women are assigned subordinate positions but fulfill functions not unlike those of mother and wife, such as wet nurses, nannies, and of course, mistresses. Freyre describes them in the following passage: "Almost all of us bear the mark of that [black] influence. Of the female slave or 'mammy' who rocked us to sleep. Who suckled us. Who fed us, mashing our food with her own hands. The influence of the old woman who told us our first tales of ghost and *bicho*. Of the mulatto girl who relieved us of our first *bicho de pé*, of a pruriency that was so enjoyable. Who initiated us into physical love and, to the creaking of a canvas cot, gave us our first sensation of being a man" (p. 278).

This passage is probably the best example in *Casa-Grande e Senzala* of the manner in which Freyre occasionally moves from the objective and even formulaic use of the third person plural to a dynamic, fluid first person that includes the reader, the narrator (Freyre), and the social group being described in its experiences: it is "we" not "they" who are raised and cared for by black and mulatto women.[20] In fact, this sporadic extension of the first person plural to include the reader serves to emphasize the paradigmatic character assigned by Freyre to the colonial family in Brazilian history. Freyre's narrative is presented not as dealing with a long-dead past, but rather as describing still existing traits relevant to any interpretation of contemporary Brazilian society.

In this passage Freyre assigns black women a central role in the physical and emotional development of white children (a group that includes the author and by implication the reader). White children are fed, tended, and entertained by black women, and their sexual maturation (characteristically described as "the first sensation of being a man") depends directly on the mulatto woman. Although socially inferior to the white mother, black and mulatto women are the central and privileged element in the libidinal and emotional economy of Freyre's patriarchal family. By stressing in his narrative the emotional centrality of black and mulatto women, however, Freyre obscures the social inequality that forces them to be servants or slaves, to care for white children, and to become the white boys' first sexual partners.

Freyre differentiates between black and mulatto women regarding the functions fulfilled within the patriarchal family. He describes black women as raising the children: "The little one was then left for the *mucamas* to raise. It was a rare case in which a Brazilian lad was not suckled by a Negro nurse and did not become more accustomed to talking to her than to his own father and mother" (p. 366). While, as slaves, mulatto women also help take care of the (white and male) "Brazilian lad," Freyre consistently emphasizes the physical and sexual aspect of their relationship with the white child and, later, man. It is the mulatto woman who initiates the adolescent boy sexually and who later becomes the lover of the plantation owner (and the victim of the white wife's jealousy; pp. 351–52). Freyre's division of the female role in the patriarchal family among black, mulatto, and white women exemplifies a racist

Brazilian saying: "A branca para casar, a mulata para fornicar, a negra para trabalhar." (The white woman for marriage, the mulatto woman for sex, the black woman for work.)

Therefore, in *Casa-Grande e Senzala,* the colonial patriarchal family is described as having a rather unusual structure. There is no doubt that the Portuguese man is the father, but the mother's role seems to be divided between white, black, and mulatto women. While the white woman is the biological mother and the legal wife, the black woman mothers the white child in terms of his emotional daily care needs, and the mulatto woman is the sexual partner of the Portuguese man (and pubescent youth).

The division of the mother/wife role in this archetypal patriarchal family limits the text's apparent celebration of mestizaje. On the one hand, there is a constant reiteration of the profound cultural, emotional, and psychological influences of black culture on the white boy/man through the role of the black mother and mulatto sexual partner. On the other, *Casa-Grande e Senzala* traces biological descent exclusively through the white mother. Despite Freyre's emphasis on mestizaje, his description of the patriarchal family as constituted by a white father and a white mother implies that miscegenation takes place only outside the family. Miscegenation is, therefore, described as taking place during the murky historical origins of this white family—when the Portuguese man took as his sexual partner the available Indian or black woman—or at the margins of the family, as the father procreates a "great multitude of illegitimate offspring" (p. 446), who are sometimes incorporated into the casa-grande.

The use of the first person plural in the passage that describes the childhood experiences of the white child also illustrates the manner in which Freyre simultaneously privileges miscegenation as the origin of Brazilian society and relegates it to the margins of the patriarchal family. By using the first person plural, the narrator assumes that the reader is male and white. Like the narrator/Freyre, the reader is assumed to have been nursed, raised, and initiated sexually by a black woman. Nowhere in that passage is there any indication that the reader may be female or may descend from the "great multitude of illegitimate offspring" or from the slaves. Although the majority of the Brazilian population is neither white nor male and does not descend from slave owners, the text implicitly describes the reader as a white male child raised by black and mulatto women. The peculiar constitution of the patriarchal family—its division of the maternal function—is incorporated into Freyre's use of the first person plural and, implicitly, places the reader in the position of a legitimate white male descendant of this family. The consequence of Freyre's assumption of a male white reader is that, while thematically *Casa-Grande e Senzala* celebrates cultural and biological mestizaje, the text rhetorically undermines this celebration. If neither the reader nor the narrator descends from blacks or Indians, it is only the "other" who is racially mixed.

If *Casa-Grande e Senzala* presents a divided, even contradictory, image of the mother in the colonial family, the role of the father is clearly described and unequivocally assigned to the Portuguese. Unlike the emasculated and feminized black and Indian males described in *Casa-Grande e Senzala,* the white Portuguese father is presented as the only procreator, as "*o membrum virile*" from whom all Brazilians descend (p. 428).

Continuities with Portugal

Unlike *Iracema* and many of the writings of the Spanish American discourse of mestizaje, which found national specificity in the representation of the Indian and Indian cultures, Freyre's narrative tends to obscure Brazil's difference from Portugal. For instance, Freyre's description of Portugal and the Portuguese resembles in its emphasis on cultural and racial hybridity his description of Brazil. Like Brazil, Portugal is described as being culturally and racially influenced by "an energetic infusion of Moorish and Negro blood, the effects of which persist to this day in the Portuguese people and the Portuguese character" (p. 211). Moreover, as in colonial Brazil, slavery is described as an institution "of which Portuguese economy had always made use" (p. 262). But for Freyre, there is an even more significant similarity between Brazil and Portugal: "Portugal in its anthropology as in its culture displays a great variety of antagonisms, some of them in a state of equilibrium, others in conflict. These latter are merely the undigested portion of its history; the major part is seen to be harmonious in its contrasts, forming a social whole that, in its plastic qualities, is characteristically Portuguese" (p. 200). As in his characterization of colonial Brazil, Freyre's description of Portuguese society also emphasizes the lack of friction between classes and races.

The question that arises, then, is what constitutes the difference between Brazil and Portugal. After all, every trait ascribed by Freyre to Brazil corresponds to a similar characteristic in his analysis of Portugal. However, Brazil is described not only in terms of the accentuation of

Portugal's characteristics, but even as the fulfillment of what is only potentially present in Portugal. If Portugal was influenced by Africa, Brazil has experienced a stronger African influence; if Portugal has a multiracial population, Brazil's population is even more so; if Portugal is characterized overall by racial and class harmony, Brazil is more harmonious; and so on. As Freyre was to emphasize in a book published seven years after *Casa-Grande e Senzala* and revealingly titled *O mundo que o Português criou* (The World the Portuguese Created) (1940): "the point of view of the author will always be that in Portugal and the various areas colonized by Portugal in America, Africa, Asia, and the islands there will always be a unity of culture and feeling. The central element for this point of view is that Portugal created many peoples that are today essentially Portuguese in their most characteristic lifestyles, and that it is in Brazil where this continuation of an older culture in a new one, more vast than the original, reached its highest intensity" (Freyre 1940, 32). Freyre's emphasis on "the unity of feeling and culture" between Portugal and Brazil in this later text is perfectly compatible with his analysis of the similarities between both countries in *Casa-Grande e Senzala*. As the word "continuation" and the phrase "highest intensity" used to describe the relationship between Portugal and Brazil in *O mundo que o Português criou* illustrate, for Freyre the difference between the two countries is one of degree, not of kind.

Casa-Grande e Senzala does not attempt to define a Brazilian national identity substantially different from that of Portugal. Freyre's lack of interest in national specificity establishes a significant difference from his predecessor José de Alencar. Although Alencar presents the colony as the foundational period when Indians and Portuguese create Brazil, he does not imply a basic similarity between Brazil and Portugal. In *Iracema,* the first Brazilian, Moacir, cannot be defined exclusively by his Portuguese heritage and, therefore, Brazil is not merely the continuation of Portugal.

Freyre's lack of interest in the development of a Brazilian identity differentiated from that of Portugal is directly related to the historical time frame in which his work is produced. Unlike Alencar, who belonged to the first generation of writers born after political independence and who was concerned with establishing a homologous cultural autonomy regarding the former metropolis, Freyre writes during a period when, while still preoccupied with problems of national identity, writers are no longer threatened by Brazil's links with Portugal. The implicit point of reference in much of *Casa-Grande e Senzala* is not Portugal but the United

States, the new cultural, political, and economic metropolis. Freyre's pre-occupation with the comparison between Brazil and the United States is found not in the few explicit references to U.S. society and history in *Casa-Grande e Senzala,* but in his representation of Brazil as a "racial democracy" (see Freyre 1956, 17, 401–2). His emphasis on the beneficial qualities of miscegenation has as its tacit counterpart the supposedly more radical exclusion of blacks and Indians from the white society of the United States.

It is important to note that Freyre's emphasis on the Portuguese filiation of Brazil is echoed by other noted Brazilian authors of his time. The other classic interpretation of Brazilian nationality produced in the 1930s, Sérgio Buarque de Holanda's *Raízes do Brasil* (1936), also emphasizes the Portuguese origin of Brazil (while marginalizing even more than Freyre does the Indian and black influences): "Neither the contact nor the mixture with indigenous or foreign races has made us as different from our grandparents from beyond the sea, as we would on occasion like to think. In the Brazilian case, the truth, no matter how unappealing to some of our patriots, is that we are still linked by a long and vibrant tradition to the Iberian Peninsula, and to Portugal in particular. This tradition is vibrant enough to feed a common soul between Brazil and Portugal despite all our differences" (Holanda [1936] 1995, 40). For Holanda, as for Freyre, Brazilian national identity is a continuation of that of Portugal.

Despite Freyre's affirmation of the Portuguese filiation of Brazil, *Casa-Grande e Senzala* still emphasizes the importance of mestizaje, both biological and cultural, in the development of the country. But Freyre's version of the discourse of mestizaje stresses in particular the role played by Africans in transforming what once was an exclusively Portuguese cultural inheritance into Brazilian culture. The Africanization of Portuguese, which is described as being the central modification of that language in Brazil, can serve as an example of the importance assigned by Freyre to mestizaje as the constitutive trait of national identity: "It was from the interpenetration of the two tendencies [Portuguese and African] that our national tongue resulted" (Freyre 1956, 347).

Not surprisingly, Freyre gives principal credit for the creation of Brazilian Portuguese to African women, who "did very often with words what she did with food; she mashed them, removed the bones, took away their hardness" (p. 343). However, as we have seen, this Brazilian specificity is shown to be simply the continuation, often the realization, of what was already present in an embryonic form in Portuguese identity. (After all, Portugal is also described by Freyre as having been influenced by Africa.) Freyre's privileging of Portugal in the formation of Brazilian identity thereby becomes compatible with his belief in the importance of mestizaje and black culture for the construction of the Brazilian nation.

Freyre's emphasis on the homology between Portugal and Brazil becomes, therefore, another means by which contradictory elements in the text are reconciled. Together with the reduction of the Brazilian population to the patriarchal family of the casa-grande, and the rhetorical identification of the narrator and reader with the white son of the same family, the near-identification of Brazil with Portugal helps domesticate the contradictions inherent in the text. In fact, one can argue that these three centripetal (in the sense that they help hold the text together) characteristics are intimately connected. By reducing the Brazilian population to the patriarchal family and assigning a semi-maternal role to blacks and Indians; by identifying the reader (and narrator) with the male white child; and finally by identifying the father as Portuguese and privileging his foundational role, all potential contradictions are eliminated from the text. Freyre manages simultaneously to be an antiracist and to defend traditional hierarchies and even colonialism.[21] Antiracism and colonialism are both compatible with defense of the black mother and the Portuguese father in *Casa-Grande e Senzala*.

Yet a price has been paid in creating a text that reconciles all social contradictions. Not only has the traditional function of the discourse of mestizaje as an attempt to ground a national identity independent from that of the metropolis and as an act of national affirmation in the face of racialist dogmas been left aside—and, therefore, any anticolonial potential eliminated from this mode of thinking—but sizable sectors of the population are eliminated from the narrative of the nation. *Casa-Grande e Senzala* ultimately becomes a defense of mestizaje directed to the Brazilian elites and especially to the male sector of that group. While nominally incorporating blacks, Indians, mestizos and mulattoes, as well as white women, *Casa-Grande e Senzala* actually excludes these sectors of the population from its discourse. Not only is the text presented as a conversation among white males, but no role is ultimately assigned to blacks, mulattoes, or Indians (except to the Indian, black, and mulatto women described as slaves and servants). And even in the case of female Indians or blacks, their role is clearly relegated to that of helping realize more fully the characteristics of harmony and hybridity already present among the (male) Portuguese. But by excluding (or subordinating to the Portuguese) the Brazilian nonwhite majority of the population from his representation of the nation, in *Casa-Grande e Senzala* Freyre actualizes the conservative potential in the discourse of mestizaje that is frequently hidden in the apparently radical rhetoric. We have already seen how this discourse almost always proposes the incorporation of Indians and blacks within a nation that is clearly the continuation of the colony. Mestizaje, therefore, implies the abandonment of most non-European cultural traits as the precondition for this incorporation into the nation. *Casa-Grande e Senzala* not only follows but exacerbates this characteristic pattern. Its genius lies in presenting the clear subordination of the nonwhite majority to a white minority as the celebration of Afro-Brazilian culture.

CHAPTER SIX

José Carlos Mariátegui

Marxist Mestizaje

José Carlos Mariátegui's critical fortune defies historical odds and intellectual fashions. Even though after his death in 1930 he became a marginal figure out of favor with the Stalinist orthodoxy that took control of the Peruvian socialist movement he had formed, today he is readily described as "perhaps the greatest Latin American Marxist" (Quijano 1995, 210).[1] What makes this about-face in the valuation of his work by the Latin American critical establishment particularly significant is that it seems to challenge the undeniable decline in the importance of Marxism in contemporary Spanish American political and intellectual life. If it is understandable that Mariátegui's brand of iconoclastic and potentially anti-Stalinist Marxism would resonate with the new left of the 1960s and 1970s, who found in him a Latin American equivalent to Antonio Gramsci, current interest in the Peruvian critic and politician requires further explanation.[2]

Part of the reason for this continued interest in the face of the radical changes in political orientation that have taken place in the last two decades can be found in the heterodox nature of Mariátegui's thought. Not bound by the Stalinist intellectual straightjacket, Mariátegui was interested in the European and North American critical, philosophical, and artistic production of his time. Not only figures that were already central to the intellectual discussion of his time (e.g., Friedrich Nietzsche or Sigmund Freud) but also lesser-known thinkers (e.g., the French syndicalist theorist Georges Sorel) exercised profound influence on Mariátegui's interpretation of Marxism.[3] Whereas the majority of his Latin American left-wing contemporaries uncritically applied the formulas proposed by the Russian-dominated Communist International in their analyses or, at best, attempted to reproduce the Marxist classics, Mariátegui saw Marxism as, to use his own words, "a heroic creation" (Mariátegui 1996, 89).

But if Mariátegui was intellectually attuned to the latest European production in philosophy, the social sciences, and literature, he was also very much a part of the Latin American intellectual tradition. It is therefore possible to see in his theoretical innovations not only the influence of European thought, but also the continuation of modes of thinking hegemonic in the Latin America of his time within a very different set of intellectual coordinates—those of Marxism. It is precisely the juxtaposition and articulation of such dissimilar intellectual discourses as Marxism and Latin American mestizaje that constitute the cornerstone of Mariátegui's effort to move beyond the dichotomies that have traditionally characterized the region's thought and literature. His Marxist version of the discourse of mestizaje permits him to override the binary oppositions between the indigenous and the Hispanic, the nativist and the cosmopolitan, or the national and the international so prevalent in Latin American cultural production.[4]

While it has been customary for critics to emphasize Mariátegui's writings as a major watershed in Peruvian and Latin American thought, in order to understand his innovations it is also necessary to analyze the less-evident continuity between his works and those of earlier Latin American thinkers. An analysis of Mariátegui's essays as part of a Latin American tradition of thinking about mestizaje leads to a fuller comprehension of his works and the recent interest in them. It is, after all, his integration of European and Latin American intellectual traditions that is at the core of the continuing preoccupation with his work. Current interest in Mariátegui is grounded not only in the possibility suggested in his writings of creating a Latin American Marxism, but also in the conjunction of European modernity and the revalorization of Amerindian cultures characteristic of his thinking and political proposals. Mariátegui is, therefore, the acknowledged or ignored prototype for later intellectuals who will attempt to find versions of modernity compatible with Latin American cultural specificity.

Underlying all of Mariátegui's writings is a profound dissatisfaction with Peruvian criollo society and its intellectuals. For him, the criollo republic of his time was the continuation of the colony and the republican elites the offspring of the colonial aristocracy. In his writings, he argues that during the republic, "the landowning aristocracy of the colony, holder of power, maintained intact its feudal rights over the land and, therefore, over the Indian" (Mariátegui [1928] 1981, 46).[5] Mariátegui believes that the continuation and flourishing of colonial social and economic structures in the republic paralleled the persistence of colonial modes of thinking. In "Literature on Trial" (1928) the seventh chapter of his *Seven Interpretive Essays* in which he reviews the Peruvian literary canon as it was understood in the 1920s, Mariátegui designates as "colonial" all Peruvian literature written by his predecessors. Unwittingly echoing Ricardo Palma's statements about his contemporaries (see chapter 3), Mariátegui proposes that only among the socially conscious intellectuals of his time are colonial modes of thinking left behind: "In the history of our literature, it is not until this generation that the colony ends and Peru finally becomes independent of the mother country" (1971, 287).[6]

For Mariátegui, José de la Riva Agüero, the most important Peruvian intellectual of the first two decades of the twentieth century, exemplifies the nostalgia for the colony typical of Peruvian thought in the republic. He describes Riva Agüero as a "descendant of the conquest" and an "heir to the colony," and presents him as the paradigmatic example of Peruvian intellectual production (p. 193). For Mariátegui, the survival of colonial characteristics in the society, culture, and politics of the republic results in both the exclusion of the Amerindians—who comprise four-fifths of the Peruvian population—from political and cultural participation, as well as the continuation of economic structures based on their exploitation.

Given this negative evaluation of the Peru of his time, Mariátegui argues that it is necessary to reject the colonial (and by extension criollo) social and cultural heritage of Peru, reconceptualize the nation from a new perspective, and transform this new vision of the nation into an alternative political, social, and cultural project. In his writings, he identifies three different but for him compatible intellectual traditions on which to found this reconceptualization of Peru. The first is the Marxist tradition, which Mariátegui discovered during his stay in Europe between 1919 and 1923.[7] The second is the national, Latin American, and international literary and artistic avant-garde movements, which according to him, provides an alternative to the cultural tradition of the criollo republic. The third is the Amerindian tradition, which he describes as characterized by the persistence of autonomous socialist practices and institutions. Although there is critical agreement that Mariátegui gave importance to these three intellectual traditions, the manner in which Marxism, the avant-garde, and the Amerindian cultural tradition are defined and articulated in his proposal of a Latin American Marxism is still a matter of controversy. Nevertheless, as numerous statements in his works (some of which will be examined in the following text) make clear, Mariátegui believed that these three intellectual traditions were profoundly interrelated and permitted the construction of an alternative conceptualization of the nation preferable to the one proposed by criollo intellectuals and politicians.

Mariátegui's Indo-American Socialism

If Marxism is a central aspect of Mariátegui's project, what he meant by this term is far from established. Despite Mariátegui's often-affirmed allegiance to and admiration for the Russian Revolution, it is difficult to characterize him intellectually and ideologically as a Marxist-Leninist. One of the peculiarities of Mariátegui's Marxism is precisely its deviance from the models proposed by the Communist International. If Marxism-Leninism is understood theoretically as constituted by dialectical and historical materialism, as well as in practice prescribing a specific political and revolutionary praxis, Mariátegui's interpretation of Marxism represents the rejection of Leninism. Dialectical materialism, a fully comprehensive philosophical interpretation of nature and social reality, is implicitly rejected in Mariátegui's refusal to see Marxism as a self-sufficient philosophy. Instead, Mariátegui argues that Marxism must be kept up to date by the incorporation of all-important philosophical or scientific innovations. While inexact as a description of mainstream Marxism, the following statement from 1929 exemplifies the degree to which Mariátegui was receptive to Western philosophical currents: "Vitalism, activism, pragmatism, relativism: none of these philosophical currents, insofar as they can bring something to the revolution, have remained marginal to the Marxist intellectual movement" (Mariátegui 1996, 151). Moreover, Mariátegui adopted Georges Sorel's concept of myth (i.e., an idea accepted in a nonrational form and capable of guiding action) as a central notion in his own conception of Marxism (see, e.g., Mariátegui 1971, 151–52; 1996, 143–45). In fact, Mariátegui not only was interested in antirational modes of thought—such as those of Henri Bergson, William James, or Sorel—but also had a keen appreciation of religion. If one remembers the anti-religious fervor characteristic of Leninism, Mariátegui's emphasis not only on the importance of religion as a historical phenomenon but on the religious nature of Marxism as a political faith exemplifies his divergence from Communist orthodoxy. It is impossible to imagine any other major Marxist thinker in the 1920s stating, "Communism is essentially religious" (Mariátegui 1971, 212).

Historical materialism, with its abstract analysis of history as a succession of modes of production that evolve in inexorable order from primitive communism to slavery, then into feudalism, then into capitalism, and finally into socialism was profoundly at odds with Mariátegui's concern for the historical and cultural specificity of Peru and Latin America.[8] Thus Mariátegui (1996, 89) states, "We certainly do not wish socialism in America to be a copy and imitation. It must be a heroic creation. We must give life to an Indo-American socialism reflecting our own reality and in our own language." Rather than the mechanical reproduction and application of the abstract formulas of international Communism, he proposed the re-creation of Marxism in Peruvian and Latin American terms.

One of Mariátegui's principal innovations was the attribution of a revolutionary potential to the Quechua and Aymara Amerindians of the Peruvian Andes. In order to evaluate how heterodox Mariátegui's position actually was, it is necessary to remember that according to Marx and Engels in the *Communist Manifesto* (1964, 75), "Of all the classes that stand face to face with the bourgeois today, the proletariat alone is a really revolutionary class." The exclusive position of the proletariat as a revolutionary class, a basic tenet of Marxism in general and of historical materialism in particular, seemed to be at odds with Mariátegui's belief in the necessity of a socialist transformation of Peruvian reality. Although the 1920s was a period of accelerated capitalist development and rapid radicalization of workers in Peru and Latin America, the Peruvian working class was numerically small and still had not become fully separated from its artisan origins (see Flores Galindo 1980, 30). Thus, in order to establish socialism in the Peru of his time, Mariátegui believed it was necessary and possible to see the Quechua and Aymara peasants as a supplementary revolutionary class.[9] Mariátegui's ascription of revolutionary capacity to the Amerindian is also based on his analysis of Peruvian reality. This belief had its roots in the numerous cycles of Indian rebellions that had marked the Andes since the conquest and that reached a particularly violent peak during the years between 1919 and 1923 as a reaction to the expansion of the *latifundios* (haciendas). The Andean Amerindians' obstinate resistance signaled for Mariátegui a revolutionary potential among the Quechua and Aymara population that needed only to be directed toward socialism. (See Mariátegui and Pesce 1996, 105 regarding the importance of Amerindian rebellions as a proof of the revolutionary potential of the Indian.)

But Mariátegui's discovery of this revolutionary possibility in the peasantry and in peasant institutions not only contradicted orthodox Marxism's privileging of the proletariat, it also denied historical materialism's fundamental belief in historical progress. According to Mariátegui's heterodox Marxism not only were Andean Amerindians potential revolutionaries, it was also possible to make the jump from the primitive communism of the *ayllu* (Andean peasant communities) to modern socialism: "The ayllu, the basic unit of the Incan state that still survives despite the attacks of feudalism and gamonalismo, summons yet enough vitality to gradually convert itself into the basic unit of a modern socialist state" (Mariátegui 1996, 86).

Mariátegui's belief in the possibility of transforming the ayllu into the central institution of a future socialist Peru, even if unthinkable within the strict framework of Marxism-Leninism, has an important precedent in the Marxist tradition. In a preface to the 1882 Russian edition of the *Communist Manifesto,* Marx himself discussed the possibility of creating a Russian socialism based on the *obschina,* the village community (Marx and Engels 1964, 124). Mariátegui was undoubtedly aware of Marx's speculations, since Sorel mentions them (Sorel 1972, 281 n. 10). But Mariátegui's complex meditation on the revolutionary implications to be found in Amerindian culture develops what in Marx is only the barest of sketches.

This revaluing of the revolutionary potential of the Amerindian also implies a modification, if not rejection, of the political organization and strategies characteristic of a Leninist Communist Party. Although individual peasants were not excluded from the Communist Party, the party's strategy, in accordance with historical materialism, was to promote a "bourgeois" revolution in a Latin America characterized as primarily feudal.[10] Mariátegui's emphasis on the possibility of achieving socialism in Peru without necessarily going through a bourgeois revolution first is based on his belief that capitalism was already present in the Peru of the 1920s, even if in an underdeveloped form. Moreover, instead of there being any type of opposition between capitalism and the *latifundistas* (landowners), a *modus vivendi* convenient to both groups had been found (Mariátegui 1971, 12–16, 21).

Indigenismo and the Avant-Garde

This discovery of the "proto-modernity" of the Amerindian as a potential revolutionary and as the creator of a socialist institution in the ayllu paralleled the discovery of the primitive as a source of modernity by many artists in the first decades of the twentieth century. Pablo Picasso's use of African masks in his celebrated painting *Les Demoiselles d'Avignon* (1907) and the presence of jazz—misinterpreted as a primitive art—in Darius Milhaud's *La creacion du monde* (1923) and Kurt Weill's and Berthold Brecht's *Three Penny Opera* (1928) illustrate the belief that in the art and culture of those populations believed to be untouched or at least little influenced by Western civilization could be found a model for a modern aesthetic. Thus, Mariátegui was able not only to discern in the Quechua and Aymara Indians a source of political modernity, but by analogy could also propose a literary and cultural practice centered on the figure of the Amerindian that did not necessarily follow nineteenth-century realist aesthetics. For Mariátegui, *indigenismo,* understood as the vindication of Amerindian culture and its values, and *vanguardismo,* the Latin American equivalent of European and North American avant-garde and modernism, were thus perfectly compatible terms. On occasion, he even wrote about "avant-garde indigenismo" (1980, 217). "This current," Mariátegui states about indigenismo, "is encouraged by the assimilation of cosmopolitan elements by our culture" ([1928] 1981, 329, my translation).[11] Indeed, Mariátegui seems to have implied that unlike the European vanguard, which had only a rhetorical relation with its primitive subject, indigenismo was much more justified in its reliance on Amerindian themes and forms because of the actual physical and historical presence and influence of the Amerindian in Peruvian society: "Indigenism . . . has its roots in the present; it finds its inspiration in the protests of millions of men" (Mariátegui 1971, 274).

The main example Mariátegui uses to illustrate his belief in the possibility of an avant-garde indigenismo is the work of Peruvian poet

César Vallejo. According to Mariátegui, Vallejo's early poems, collected as *Los heraldos negros* (1918), "probably mark the beginning of Peruvian, in the sense of indigenous, poetry" (p. 251). According to Mariátegui, Vallejo is a mestizo who expresses in his poetry the emotional ties he maintains with his Amerindian heritage (p. 250). Thus, Mariátegui claims to find what he considers to be distinctive Amerindian characteristics, such as pessimism and nostalgia, in Vallejo's poetry (pp. 252–54). In Mariátegui's analysis, the Amerindian characteristics are precisely those that determine Vallejo's modernity. For instance, the symbolist filiation of Vallejo's early writings, which could be attributed to the influence of the European poetic school, is seen instead as additional proof of the persistence of the poet's Amerindian heritage: "The symbolist style is better suited than any other to interpret the indigenous spirit. Being animist and rustic, the Indian tends to express himself in anthropomorphic or pastoral images" (pp. 251–52). Likewise, Mariátegui interprets the emphasis in Vallejo's poetry on the "human condition" over the expression of the individual emotions and experiences of the poetic persona as a link with both modernity and the Amerindian: "The romanticism of the nineteenth century was basically individualistic; the romanticism of the 1900s is, on the other hand, spontaneous and logically socialist, unanimist. Vallejo from this point of view, belongs not only to his race but also to his century, to his era" (p. 256). For Mariátegui, Vallejo proves that modernity and indigenismo are not only compatible, but that in the context of Peru they are also necessarily linked. As Mariátegui (1996, 72) writes about nationalism and literature: "The most national in any literature is always the most profoundly revolutionary." In Mariátegui's writings, the national element in literature, redefined as centered around the Amerindian tradition, and the "revolutionary" element, which includes the European and North American avant-garde as well as the literature inspired by radical politics, become fused. Mariátegui's analysis of indigenismo as both a sociopolitical and artistic movement exemplifies the conjunction of the political and the literary, and of the national and the revolutionary, typical of his work. In Mariátegui's thought, indigenismo plays a particularly important political role since it leads to the superseding of the colonialist culture that, according to him, characterized the Peru of his time: "Indigenism, as we have seen, is gradually uprooting colonialism" (1971, 287). By helping to destroy the colonialist criollo culture and literature, which functioned as the ideological justification for the political system that exploited the

Amerindian, indigenismo fulfills an important, even revolutionary, political function.

In Mariátegui's thought, artistic revolution, political revolution, and the vindication of the Amerindian end up becoming if not identical, at least profoundly intertwined with each other. It is not accidental that his important 1925 essay "Nationalism and Vanguardism" (in Mariátegui 1996) is divided into separate studies that analyze the relationship of both nationalism and the avant-garde first to the politics and then to the arts of Peru. But even as Mariátegui separates the aesthetic from the political in his analysis, he implicitly recognizes their interrelationship by including the two studies as sections of the same essay.

The Amerindian Tradition

The cornerstone in Mariátegui's intellectual edifice is the Andean Amerindian. Mariátegui assigns the Andean Amerindian a central role in the political, economic, aesthetic, and cultural proposals with which he attempts to replace the structures, institutions, and culture of the Peru of his time. In Mariátegui's political proposals, the Amerindian is a principal revolutionary agent. In the aesthetic field, Mariátegui proposes the Amerindian not only as the subject matter of literary and artistic works but, because of the compatibility established between Amerindian culture and the international avant-garde, also as a formal influence on the creation of modern works of art. The result of bringing Andean Amerindian cultural values to the forefront is, as we have seen, the undermining of the colonialist ideology that he sees as buttressing the unjust social and economic structures of Peru. Furthermore, since Mariátegui believes that Andean Amerindian institutions, such as the ayllu, possess the potential to become important elements of a future modern socialist nation, his interpretation of Marxism can be read as a radical version of social indigenismo. In sum, the importance of the Andean Amerindian in Mariátegui's work is such that it implies a change from earlier conceptualizations of Peru as basically a criollo nation to one centered on the Amerindian tradition.

Nevertheless, when proposing the centrality of Amerindian traditions, Mariátegui repeats many of the arguments of earlier and contemporary nonrevolutionary versions of mestizaje. For instance, Mariátegui sees Peruvian nationality as an unfinished project grounded in the Amerindian: "We definitely know that, regarding Peru, this concept [nationality] will not be created without the Indian. The Inca past has been incorporated into our history vindicated not by the traditionalists but by the revolutionaries. This is the key to the defeat of a colonialism that still survives, in part, as a social situation—feudalism, latifundism—but is defeated forever in spirit. The revolution has vindicated our oldest tradition" (Mariátegui 1981b, 121).

Mariátegui adds an important modification to this characteristic use of the Indian: the same gesture that grounds the nation also grounds socialism. He believes that "the Indian, in spite of one hundred years of republican legislation, has not become an individualist" (1971, 57). By identifying Amerindian culture as socialist, Mariátegui describes the future Peruvian socialism not only as compatible with Andean Amerindian culture and values, but even as based at least in part on those values. As we have seen, he proposed that Indian institutions such as the ayllu would play a major role in a socialist future that would include, as one of its central measures, land reform intended to reinforce Andean agrarian socialism.[12] Indeed, Mariátegui establishes a clear continuity between national past and future, since the Inca Empire and a socialist Peru are both defined as based on Amerindian institutions. But he also establishes a similar continuity between socialism and the "true" Peruvian nation, given that both are to be built around socialist cultural traditions attributed to the Amerindians. The Spanish colony and the criollo republic appear in this conceptualization as a brief foreign interlude in a national and cultural continuity that stretches back hundreds of years or more before the conquest and looks forward to a socialist future that, one assumes, is also expected to endure. In spite of the undeniable originality of Mariátegui's conjunction of socialism and the nation, his innovations have to be seen as personal appropriations of the discourse of mestizaje. After all, conceptualizations of the nation based on mestizaje frequently see the colonial period as a moment of foreign domination that divided a national Indian period from a national republican one.[13]

Mariátegui's linking of socialism and the nation is probably one of his principal contributions to a Latin American Marxism that has often equated nationalism with revolution. The imbrication of socialism and the nation implies, however, another major departure from Marxist-Leninist orthodoxy. Marx and Engels (1964, 90) had unambiguously declared that "workingmen have no country." They also believed that capitalism was quickly erasing national differences, and that economic and cultural internationalization would accelerate under the "supremacy of the proletariat" (p. 90). In 1913, Joseph Stalin, writing under Lenin's direction, produced the classic Marxist-Leninist study of the problem of nationalism, "Marxism and the National Question." While Stalin in this text deviated from most previous Marxist thought by emphasizing the importance of the nation and nationalism, he conditioned the response of the Communist movement toward the national aspirations of specific groups on the "interests of the toiling masses" (Stalin 1975, 39). For Stalin there was no immutable rule to be applied to national claims; the Communist Party was to evaluate each individual national case and decide whether to support or oppose autonomy, federation, or separation based on the party's own revolutionary interests (p. 39).

Despite some superficial similarities between their analyses of nationalism, Mariátegui's position differs substantially from Stalin's. Although, like Stalin, Mariátegui emphasizes the relative nature of national claims, for him there is a clear difference between nationalism in the developed world, where it is linked to the political right and to imperialism, versus that of the colonial nations where "nationalism is revolutionary, and, therefore, concludes in socialism" (Mariátegui 1980, 221). Mariátegui identifies nationalism with revolution in the colonial nations because he believes that only socialism is anti-imperialist and capable of successfully struggling to eliminate colonial oppression. Nonrevolutionary nationalisms are ultimately co-opted by the possibility of higher wages for the local elites provided by transnational corporations (Mariátegui 1996, 135). This identification between nationalism and socialism in the so-called Third World contradicts the clear differentiation established by Stalin (1975, 88–96) between national and revolutionary movements.

In fact, the Comintern, acting on the behalf of the "toiling masses," had already decided that the Quechua and Aymara in the Andean countries constituted a separate nation (Flores Galindo 1980, 31–32). Not surprisingly, Mariátegui opposed this decision because he believed the achievement of Indian national claims would lead to the reproduction of capitalist relations in the new Amerindian nation (Mariátegui and Pesce 1980, 80–81). However, one can safely conclude that the fact that these claims contradict his conceptualizations of the nation and of socialism is of equal importance in his position. Although Mariátegui's analysis of a Peruvian society divided between a criollo coastal minority and an Andean Indian majority was arguably congruent with claims of nationhood for the Andean populations, his vision of the Peruvian nation and of socialism as being based on the Amerindian made it necessary for him to oppose the division of the country. If Mariátegui accepted the notion of an autonomous national and political project for the Andean Amerindian, the articulation he made between socialism and the Peruvian national tradition would become invalid. Mariátegui could propose that nationalism and socialism should be considered not only as compatible, but also as virtually synonymous, precisely because both the nation and the socialist future are based on the Amerindian. Mariátegui's thought can be interpreted as an extension of the discourse of mestizaje from the field of national identity and history into that of socialism and intellectual production. Mariátegui proposes a mestizo nationalism, socialism, and avant-garde, as well as a mestizo nation.

The Contradictions in Marxist Mestizaje

But if the discourse of mestizaje has been shown to conclude in a series of aporias, such as that between the purported assimilation of the Amerindians and their effective marginalization, one must question whether the same is true of Mariátegui's socialist version of the discourse of mestizaje. If one takes Mariátegui's conjunction of the Amerindian tradition, socialism, and the avant-garde as the central characteristic of his thought, it becomes necessary to examine the way in which each of these terms is conceptualized in his work and whether there is a hidden hierarchy structuring the relations among these terms.

Despite Mariátegui's emphasis on the revolutionary potential of Andean Amerindian culture and population, his evaluation of other Amerindian groups is much less positive. In fact, he establishes a hierarchy among Amerindian groups in which, with the possible exception of the Amerindians of Mexico and Central America that he identifies as "Aztec," the Andean Quechua and Aymara are seen as superior to other Indian groups (Mariátegui and Pesce 1980, 49). For instance, in his "El destino de Norteamérica" (1927), Mariátegui analyzes the colonization of North America in terms that differ substantially from his characteristic criticism of the Spanish colony and that imply a negative evaluation of the North American Indian: "On the virginal land of America, from which they erased all Indian tracks, the Anglo-Saxon colonizers set the basis of the capitalistic order from their arrival" (Mariátegui 1981a, 148, my translation).[14] What is of interest in this passage is the contradictory notion of a land that is virginal—that is, untouched by humanity—and at the same time marked by the "tracks" of its Amerindian population. In fact, if one defines "virginal land" as country that has been neither explored nor cultivated, two accepted meanings of the Spanish phrase, Mariátegui's misrepresentation of North American Indian cultures and peoples becomes obvious.[15] After all, it was the Amerindians' knowledge of the geography of North America and their mastery of the kind of agriculture appropriate to the different climates of the continent that made possible both English colonization and, later, American expansion toward the Pacific. There is also a demeaning connotation in the use of the word "virginal" to describe the land, since it implies that the Amerindian was incapable of possessing—one could even say deflowering—the North American landscape. The sexual connotation of this passage becomes clearer when one compares it with Mariátegui's description in his *Seven Interpretive Essays* of the establishment of the English colonies: "The Anglo-Saxon colonizer did not find in North America an advanced culture or a potent population."[16] The use of another word laden with sexual connotations—potent—to emphasize the small population—which one can assume is itself a consequence of this implied lack of potency—is significant. The quotation gives Amerindian "impotence" as the reason for the immaculate state of the North American land. Moreover, this impotence, resulting in a small Amerindian population unable to permanently modify or mark the natural environment, appears in both passages to validate the colonization of North America by the Anglo-Saxons, who are described as rapidly building a new and superior society. In fact, repeating one of the characteristic images found in colonialist texts, the *Seven Interpretative Essays* contains passages where the Amerindian presence disappears altogether from Mariátegui's description of North America, and the British colonization is presented as the simple taking over of an empty land. In the case of the British colonization of North America, Mariátegui (1971, 143) claims that "a territory, rather than a culture and a people, had to be conquered." It is symptomatic of his positive appraisals of North American colonization that Mariátegui, who so eloquently criticized the conquest of Peru as a "tremendous butchery" ([1928] 1981, 44), describes the genocide of the North American Indians as a gentle "erasing of tracks," if not as the taking over of unpopulated territory.

Mariátegui's brief references to the Amerindians of the Amazon are similar to those to the North American Indians. In Mariátegui's analysis the jungle area of Peru, populated by "primitive" Amerindian groups, is also described as empty. In *Seven Interpretive Essays,* he writes about the Peruvian population as divided exclusively between those living on the coast and those living in the Andean regions (1971, 162–64). In fact, no mention is made of the Amazonian Amerindians in the *Seven Interpretive Essays.* In a later text co-authored with Hugo Pesce, "El problema de las razas en América Latina" (1929), the nomadic and "primitive" lifestyles of the Amazonian Amerindians are characterized as "the opposite of that of the Incaic Indians" (Mariátegui and Pesce 1980, 50). Moreover, when studying the "racial problem" in Brazil, Mariátegui and Pesce describe the Amazonian Indians as being inassimilable into the socialist movement (p. 52). One can conclude that for Mariátegui the numerically few and technologically backward Amerindians of the Amazon, like those of North America, are incapable of "marking the land," and therefore exist outside history.

Of all the descriptions of racial and ethnic groups in Mariátegui's works none is more consistently negative than the description of blacks. Unlike the Andean Indians, whom he identifies with socialism, blacks are linked with what he considers the most antinational and politically and culturally retrograde period in the nation's history, the colony: "Blacks, mulattoes, and *zambos* represent colonial elements in our past" (Mariátegui [1928] 1981, 333, my translation).[17] In fact, Mariátegui's statements repeat the stereotypes of nineteenth-century racialism, describing blacks as possessing a "false servility" and as having "hot, tropical blood" (1971, 272).

Mariátegui's dismissive descriptions of blacks, non-Andean Amerindians, and Chinese raise the disturbing question of whether he was a racist.[18] In order to consider this question, one must first take into account the fragmentary character of much of his writing. Mariátegui's works consist mostly of quickly written journalistic essays that, with the exception of *Seven Interpretive Essays* and *La escena contemporánea* (1925), were not collected into books in his lifetime.[19] Thus, although one can find passages in his writings that repeat the stereotypes of racialist thinking, the totality of his work implies a rebuttal of racialism. Mariátegui (1971, 25) is aware that "the concept of inferior races was useful to the white man's West for purposes of expansion and conquest." Mariátegui still classifies human groups in a hierarchy, but one based on culture rather than race: "Racial prejudice has diminished; but the progress of sociology and history has broadened and strengthened the idea that there are differences and inequalities in the evolution of people. Although the inferiority of colored races is no longer one of the dogmas that sustain a battered white pride, all of the relativism of today does not suffice to abolish cultural inferiority" (p. 280). Thus, in spite of occasional racist remarks, Mariátegui's discriminatory comments are ultimately grounded in cultural considerations. Culture becomes for Mariátegui the ultimate criterion by which social, ethnic, or racial groups are evaluated. But Mariátegui's emphasis on culture as a determinant of human behavior also implies that a change in the cultural environment may result in a modification of the characteristics of human groups. For instance, according to Mariátegui, blacks, whom he had described as backward elements in society, can become productive members of society by embracing socialism, which through "awakening in him [the black person] a class consciousness, can lead him to break with the last traces of colonial spirit" ([1928] 1981, 334, my translation).[20] For Mariátegui, the cultural change implied in the adoption of socialism leads to a modification in a person's behavior and modes of thinking. In a similar manner, Mariátegui, who does not value the cultural contributions of Chinese immigrants to Peru, has great admiration for the achievements of the Asian countries of his time: "The people of Asia, who are in no way superior to the Indians, have not needed any transfusion of European blood in order to assimilate the most dynamic and creative aspects of Western culture" (1971, 25). In Mariátegui's reasoning, therefore, Asians are not permanently classified as an inferior group but, because of the modernization of Asian nations, can be presented as an example to be followed by Peru. In fact, as this passage makes clear, the success of Asians in adopting Western culture is presented as an argument against racial determinism.

Nevertheless, Mariátegui is not completely free from racialist dogma. While his arguments explicitly propose the possibility of changing human nature through the modification of the cultural and economic environment, in his writings he also claims to believe in race as a secondary but still relevant factor for the explanation of human behavior (p. 280). In fact, Mariátegui frequently juxtaposes in his writings an egalitarian argument with a racial stereotype or vice versa, even though racial considerations are not only marginal to his core arguments, but actually contradict them. There are even passages in Mariátegui's works where one can find a rebuttal of racialism juxtaposed with the justification of racist ideas.[21]

Mariátegui, despite his contradictions, rejects scientific racialism, but is unable to fully leave behind the racist beliefs and stereotypes that this pseudoscience justified. Furthermore, Mariátegui's work is of interest because it makes explicit the racism underlying much thinking about culture from the 1920s to the present. In fact, it is possible to see in aspects of Mariátegui's writings an early, and undeniably unwilling, precedent for the cultural racism of much of the current European right.[22]

An important example of Mariátegui's contradictions and his oscillations between racism and what could be called culturalism can be found in his analysis, in *Seven Interpretive Essays,* of José Vasconcelos's theory of the cosmic race; that is, the belief that generalized miscegenation would lead to the overcoming of social and ethnic divisions. Mariátegui bases his evaluation of the cosmic race on his interpretation of the history of miscegenation in Peru. In spite of the similarity between Mariátegui's Latin American Marxism and theories of the nation based on the discourse of mestizaje, he is very pessimistic about the contributions that the different ethnic groups have made—and can make—to Peruvian society. Mariátegui finds, as we have seen, the presence of blacks and Chinese in Peruvian society to be negative since, for him, both groups possess cultures too primitive or decrepit to contribute anything of value to the country (pp. 279–80). He also finds the contribution of the mestizos to be negligible: "Neither European nor Indian tradition is perpetuated in the mestizo; they sterilize each other" (p. 282). Unlike racialist thinkers, Mariátegui does not attribute this decline of the mestizo to biological degeneration, but rather to the stifling characteristics of Peruvian society: "In the lethargy of the feudal latifundium and the backward town, the virtues and values of racial intermixture are nullified and replaced by debilitating superstitions" (p. 282).

Not surprisingly, Mariátegui excludes Quechua and Aymara Amerindians from this negative evaluation of the social contributions made by ethnic groups in Peru. As we know, Mariátegui valued Andean Amerindian traditions for their compatibility, if not identification, with socialism, but in the following passage, he gives an additional reason: Andean Amerindian culture is described as organic. While blacks and Chinese, who were brought to Peru as slaves or indentured peasants, are seen as being extraneous elements in the national society, Mariátegui describes the Quechua and Aymara Amerindians as constituting an "organic type of society" fully integrated with their environment and possessing a continuous and autonomous history (p. 283). And for Mariátegui it is precisely this organic characteristic of a society that makes possible the assimilation of modernity, which is of central importance to his thought.

Of particular significance is the persistence of the traditional Western cultural hierarchy in Mariátegui's discussion of miscegenation. In his analysis, "white" Europe and North America are presented as constituting the norm against which Peru—and its heterogeneous population—is to be measured. Since Europe is described in terms of technological and industrial modernity, Mariátegui reintroduces in his arguments the valorization of historical progress that in other aspects of his thought he apparently rejects: "What is important, therefore, in a sociological study of the Indian and mestizo strata is not the degree to which the mestizo inherits the qualities or defects of the progenitor races, but his ability to evolve with more ease than the Indian toward the white man's social state or type of civilization" (p. 281). Mariátegui criticizes criollo and Spanish cultures precisely for their inability to create a modern, developed, and industrial nation. Unlike criollo Peru, with its latifundios and "backward" cities, Europe is described as "a mechanized civilization that is amazingly equipped to dominate nature" (p. 282). Moreover, Mariátegui privileges Western European civilization by presenting industrial development as the necessary condition for the constitution of a unified Peruvian nation out of the country's heterogeneous population: "But this process of assimilation and incorporation is quickly accomplished only within a vigorous industrial culture" (p. 282).

The positive revaluation of the Amerindian, rightfully seen as one of Mariátegui's major achievements, is also problematized by his privileging of European and North American industrial civilization. In fact, Mariátegui values Andean Indian culture because it shares an organic quality with Asian countries such as Japan, Turkey, and China, which in Mariátegui's view "proved to us that even after a long period of collapse, an autochthonous society can rapidly find its own way to modern civilization and translate into its own tongue the lessons of the West" (p. 283). Surprisingly, the Quechua and Aymara cultures are valued because in their organicity they are seen as making possible the reproduction of Western industry and culture, even if modified by a "translational process." Thus, the goal for Mariátegui is the transformation of Peru into a national—that is, Amerindian—version of modernity.

Despite Mariátegui's rightful claim to being a Marxist and a socialist, his version of socialism privileges European and North American industrial society as a goal to be achieved in Peru and Latin America. For Mariátegui, the failure of the Peruvian criollo bourgeoisie to achieve modernization justifies socialism. Throughout his writings he emphasizes the collusion of the Peruvian bourgeoisie with the landowner class, and the subordination of both to North American and English capital, as the reasons why capitalism in Peru is structurally incapable of modernizing the country (pp. 12–21, 69–70). Socialism becomes, therefore, the only means Peru has to achieve a version of industrial civilization. Because the structural deficiencies of the Peruvian economy, described by Mariátegui as a stable articulation of capitalistic and precapitalistic elements, made the elimination of the semifeudal agrarian structure impossible, socialism becomes the only feasible alternative for modernizing the country. Mariátegui's goal frequently seems to be a modern industrial socialist society, rather than merely a socialist one.

In fact, modernity can be interpreted as the unifying factor accounting for the importance given to the avant-garde, socialism, and the Andean Amerindian cultural tradition in Mariátegui's thought. These three elements are valued because they are modern or, in the case of Quechua and Aymara cultures, because they have the potential to become modern. Mariátegui's emphasis on modernity becomes particularly problematic in the case of the Amerindian. Whereas in earlier versions of the discourse of mestizaje, Amerindian cultures (especially pre-Columbian ones) are valued precisely for being potentially national, in Mariátegui's analysis it is their socialist traits, and particularly their potential modernity, that determines their importance. By being proto-socialist, the Amerindian not only grounds the nation and socialism, but also makes modernity possible.

Mariátegui, therefore, reproduces a characteristic aporia of the discourse of mestizaje as a national ideology: the use of the Indian in a national project defined by the criollo elites. Mariátegui differs from these earlier versions of this discourse in that both socialism and modernity are included in his definition of the nation. In fact, the possibility of nationhood seems to depend on the achievement of modernity while the possibility of modernity depends, in turn, on socialism. If, for Mariátegui, the past "disperses, isolates, separates, differentiates in excess the elements of nationality" (1981, 24), the future industrial civilization leads to the "assimilation and incorporation" of the different ethnic and racial groups (1971, 282).

Mariátegui's criticism of criollo Peru is, therefore, linked to this group's inability to develop the modern industrial society necessary to incorporate all ethnic groups and create a modern, homogeneous nation. Because Amerindians are seen as proto-socialist, and therefore proto-modern, Mariátegui sees in them the possibility of creating a nation that, by being both modern and socialist, is able to achieve this goal. The Quechua and Aymara are valued not for their specific cultural values, but for the possibility they offer for a future constitution of the nation.

Mariátegui's political and cultural proposals thus both echo and contradict earlier conceptualizations of the nation rooted in the discourse of mestizaje. In fact, Mariátegui is critical of the effects of miscegenation and even of cultural hybridity in the concrete case of Peru. He believes that the actual results of the miscegenation of the Peruvian population have not been positive. Nor does he present the mestizo as an example of "Peruvianness." Nevertheless, in his attempts to ground socialism within Peruvian history and population, Mariátegui resorts to the Amerindian in a manner reminiscent of earlier examples of the discourse of mestizaje. Mariátegui thus becomes a prime example of the power of this discursive tradition to capture even those who claim to be in opposition to it.

In spite of its contradictory aspects, Mariátegui's thought implies a profound innovation in Peruvian and Latin American intellectual production. Unlike earlier versions of the discourse of mestizaje that were concerned principally with establishing an independent historical basis for the nation, Mariátegui's thought emphasizes the contributions of the contemporary Andean Amerindians. Thus, he found in the existing cultural values and institutions of these people, such as the ayllu, central contributions to a future Peruvian socialism.

Moreover, even if marked by Eurocentrism, Mariátegui's reflections on the possibility of an alternative road to modernity have played a pioneering role in Latin American thought. In the 1920s Mariátegui postulated the inability of underdeveloped capitalism to create equitable societies, and he attempted to find an alternative. One could argue, in fact, that elements of Eurocentrism are implicit in the concept of an alternative modernity, and that present in the search for a different route to economic and cultural modernization is a hierarchy that privileges the European and North American societies, where modernity originated, over traditional ones. Traditional cultures, at best, are presented as possessing elements that may be able to supplement modernity or ameliorate modernization's undesirable consequences. In its contradictions and achievements, Mariátegui's work can thus be read as an early and influential precursor to later attempts at conceiving alternative versions of modernity formulated by writers dissatisfied with the social and cultural results of capitalism in Latin America. And, thus we arrive at another reason for Mariátegui's relevance to today's intellectual climate.

The problems Mariátegui tackled in his works continue to be alive in the Latin America of the twenty-first century. Like him, contemporary Latin Americans are still attempting to find political and social alternatives capable of reconciling the national and the international, the mestizo and indigenous cultures, with modernity, and of achieving the elusive twin goals of social justice and economic development. Mariátegui, therefore, can be seen as a prototype that many later Latin American thinkers have willingly or unwittingly followed.

Furthermore, if Mariátegui's identification of socialism, modernity, and nationalism—that is, his proposal of socialism as a means to achieve a modern, industrial, and integrated nation—can be taken as his principal contribution to later Latin American Marxism, his emphasis on contemporary Amerindian institutions becomes his central legacy to Latin American literature. It is not accidental that the major indigenista novels of César Vallejo, Ciro Alegría, and José María Arguedas would follow Mariátegui's lead by concentrating on the relationship between Amerindian culture and modernity. In fact, as I will show in chapter 9, it is José María Arguedas who in his novels, short stories, and essays continues, develops, and problematizes Mariátegui's search for an alternative modernity reconciled with Quechua and Aymara cultural values.

CHAPTER SEVEN

The Black Song of Los Van Van

Afrocentrism, the Discourse of Mestizaje, and Postrevolutionary Cuban Identity

Los Van Van are not only Cuba's most popular dance band, they are also its most controversial. For many Cuban Americans, they personify the hated revolution. Miami Mayor Joe Carollo has even called them "the official communist band of Fidel Castro" (Castillo 1999, 37). Their concert in Miami in 1999 gave rise to demonstrations where between 3,500 and 4,000 people waved signs reading "Cuba sí, Van Van no" and pelted the two thousand concertgoers with rocks, bottles, and eggs (Garcia, Levin, and Whoriskey 1999, 1).

Regardless of how one judges the actions of the demonstrators, the association of Los Van Van with the revolutionary government is not unfounded: the band's name comes from the slogan "diez millones y van" (ten million and going) popularized during the 1969 sugar harvest in reference to the Cuban government's goal of harvesting ten million tons of sugarcane (Mauleon and Faro 1999, 9). In the 1989 song "No soy de la gran escena," which answers their highbrow critics, Los Van Van make explicit their identification with the revolution.

But the linkage of Los Van Van with the revolution is not absolute. If Cuban revolutionary identity has frequently depended on the postulation of the United States as the enemy, this opposition is partially undermined in the case of Los Van Van. The name Los Van Van is not only a reference to a famous moment—and catchphrase—of the Cuban Revolution; it is also a translation of the English phrase "go-go" (Mauleon and Faro 1999,

9). The band's name becomes, therefore, not only a signifier for revolutionary identity, but also for the traces of U.S. pop and rock to be found in the band's music. The name that aligns the band with the Cuban Revolution also aligns them with the music and culture of the United States.[1] Paradoxically, the dance band of the Cuban Revolution, for some a symbol of Communist nationalism, has also been classified as a rock and roll band (Fernández 1988).

This simultaneous presence of Cuba and the United States becomes even more evident in Los Van Van's first U.S. production, the Grammy Award–winning *Llegó Van Van/Van Van Is Here* (1999). While the bilingual title obviously serves a commercial purpose by addressing both an existing Spanish-speaking and potential English-speaking audience, the reference to change of location merits further analysis. Given that the commercial release of the recording was timed to coincide with one of Los Van Van's recent tours of North America, it is possible to identify the "here" of the title with the United States. *Llegó Van Van/Van Van Is Here* seems to imply that Los Van Van, like many other Cubans before them, have come to the United States. It is arguably not too much of a stretch to find in the title an appeal to Cuban American audiences that, as we will see, is consistent with the postrevolutionary version of Cuban identity presented in their recent records.

In *Llegó Van Van/Van Van Is Here,* this reconceptualization of Cuban identity is best exemplified by "Somos cubanos" (1999), composed by Samuel Formell, the son of Juan Formell, the band's founder and leader. In fact, the song begins with a statement of its underlying purpose: "So that the world knows the reason for our Cuban flavor."[2]

"Somos cubanos" (1999), like most attempts at grounding national identity, is based on a historical narrative (even if mistaken in its chronology):

> In 1400 Columbus arrived
> And discovered this beautiful island
> Where the Indian race lived
> Which in due time he exterminated
> The African race arrived
> And they mixed it with the Spanish
> The mulatto woman was born

La cubana[3] [The Cuban woman/race/culture]
It was a different mixture
With a lot of swing

Cuban difference is here based on the biological fusion among the groups that make up the Cuban population. In "Somos cubanos," Los Van Van are, therefore, tapping into the Latin American tradition of finding in miscegenation the origin of national identity. As we know, rather than presenting racial and cultural heterogeneity as disrupting social unity, the discourse of mestizaje argues that this plurality is precisely what permits the constitution of the nation through genetic and cultural fusion. "We are the perfect mixture / the purest combination" is how the song expresses this paradoxical notion of racial and cultural diversity leading to identity (a word derived from the Latin word for sameness).

However, an analysis of the lyrics of "Somos cubanos" presents some significant deviations from conventional conceptualizations of Cuban history and identity as based on the fusion of African and Spanish populations. Despite the definition of Cuba as being born out of the mixture of the African and Spanish races—and the contradictory claim in the chorus of being at the same time "Cuban, Spaniard, and African"—"Somos cubanos" de-emphasizes Spanish and Hispano-Cuban elements in its version of national identity. In this manner, Los Van Van go beyond the frequent formulaic acknowledgment of the mulattoization, or Afro-Hispanic nature, of Cuban history and culture. Instead, they present an Afrocentric narrative that is the basis of the postrevolutionary version of identity found in *Llegó Van Van/Van Van Is Here*.

As befits a song that, like all of Los Van Van's songs, firmly belongs to the Afro-Cuban tradition, the lyrics of "Somos cubanos" place special stress on music as a central element of national identity. In the lyrics, the Cuban "different mixture" is "accompanied by the rumba and the *guaguancó*," two of the most traditional Afro-Cuban musical genres. Moreover, Cuban difference is described as grounded not only in miscegenation but also in black musical traditions, in particular the *clave* and its rhythms: "Masters of the *clave* / And the magic of the three plus two / That made us so special."[4]

Los Van Van's Afrocentric version of identity is further developed in the lyrics sung by Mario Rivera but not included in the booklet that accompanies the compact disc.[5] In a gesture that balances the previous mention of the mulata as the end product of Cuban miscegenation, a section of these lyrics is addressed to a *negrito* who is also the protagonist of the song's narrative. Here and in the earlier mention of the mulata, Los Van Van are referring to stock figures of national identity. During the late-nineteenth-century wars of independence, the characters of the mulata and the negrito began to be used in the *teatro vernáculo* (Cuban vaudeville) as representations of nationality (Moore 1997, 132–35, 143–46).[6] This inscription of nationalist meanings into what had until then been simply racist comical stereotypes made the mulata and the negrito ambiguous signifiers of race and nation. As Robin D. Moore (1997, 44) notes, "Afro-Cuban characters continued to serve as objects of public ridicule, and yet for the first time they also represented Cuba itself." By eliminating any comic connotations from their use of the figures of the negrito and the mulata, Los Van Van purge these characters of their traditional ambiguity. Through the figure of the negrito, "Somos cubanos," further develops its Afrocentric version of national history and identity. The song now traces Cuba's history beyond its discovery, the extermination of the Amerindians, and the foundational moment of black and white miscegenation:

> Wild forest
> Dancing negrito
> Escape to the forest
> Hide in the deep forest
> There is your protection
> In the wild forest
> Black *cimarrón* [fugitive slave]

By presenting the negrito as the person listening and dancing to the song ("dancing negrito") and simultaneously as the protagonist of the historical narrative (the cimarrón who seeks protection in the wilderness) black Cubans are figured as past and current protagonists of the country's history. If earlier versions of national identity imply narratives of acculturation into criollo culture and national projects, Los Van Van present one in which mestizaje leads to the negrito—Cuba's black population—and the hegemony of Afro-Cuban traditions.

Given this identification of Cubans with the negrito, the recurring references in the song to Afro-Cuban religion are not surprising. Santería (Afro-Cuban religion) has always been at the core of black Cuban life.[7] In the song, the negrito is defended by los santos (African deities). He is called "son of Changó" and "*obbariosiaero.*" (Obbá is an African deity.)

"Somos cubanos" is not the only song on *Llegó Van Van/Van Van Is Here* where references are made to Santería. In the first song of the compact disc, "Permiso que llegó Van Van" it is claimed that "los santos" sing in praise of Los Van Van, in this manner granting divine approval to their implicit geographical relocation. This emphasis on Santería as one of the sources of Cuban identity is, however, even more intensely expressed in a song originally recorded in 1996, "Soy todo." There, it is explicitly stated that Cuban identity is grounded in Santería.

Los Van Van's stress on Santería as central to the country's identity is a break with earlier Cuban discourse on the nation both before and after the revolution. The Cuban avant-garde of the 1920s and 1930s, like their counterparts throughout the world, had been interested in African cults mainly as a rich source for images and sounds, which they translated into the artistic languages of modernity. And, while some have spoken about the revolutionary government's "official policy of not only recognizing, but embracing the country's rich Afro-Cuban heritage—especially music and dance" (Manuel 1991, 308), Santería has at best been tolerated. In 1979, Rogelio Furé, an intellectual aligned with the Cuban Revolution, described the government's goal as the gradual elimination of Afro-Cuban religion, defined as "superstition, taboos without scientific basis, medical quackery, coprolagia, xenophobia, magical conceptions about supernatural forces which govern people's lives, etc." (Furé 1991, 258–59).

By fusing religion and nationality, history and music, in "Somos cubanos" Los Van Van go beyond the somewhat cosmetic Afrocentrism of both the Cuban avant-garde and the revolution. However, this emphasis on African religious tradition as central to Cuban identity corresponds closely to the social changes that have taken place on the island. Moore (1997, 226) comments, "In the 1990s, African-derived religious expression has become if anything more widely practiced than in the past."

By means of the figure of the negrito, Los Van Van incorporate and modify the meanings associated with Cuban historical events and cultural products. An example of this semantic modification is Rivera's quotation of the titular verse of Silvio Rodríguez's classic *nueva trova* song from 1978, "La era está pariendo un corazón" (the era is giving birth to a heart; S. Rodríguez 1991).[8]

With its references to armed struggle in both country and city, Rodríguez's song is both a call and an extended metaphor for revolution. "La era está pariendo un corazón" implies a Hegelian/Marxian narrative in which revolutionary struggle and the resulting utopia are presented as the end—in every meaning of the word—of history. But in "Somos cubanos" Los Van Van present the negrito as the solution to the enigmatic first verse: "The era is giving birth to a heart / And it's you, negrito." Thus, the Cuban Revolution and the nueva trova, its representative musical genre, are seen as moments in the history of black Cubans. By appropriating Rodriguez's titular verse, Los Van Van show the negrito and Afrocentric Cuba as inheriting the utopian connotations of the original nueva trova song.

In "Somos cubanos" Los Van Van also make reference to exile and migration. The song claims that "wherever we go we make things good." "Somos cubanos" not only mentions the emigration of Cubans in a positive light, but also includes the Cuban exodus in its narrative of nationality. Exile and revolution, the two opposing poles of Cuban experience in the last forty years, are part of Los Van Van's story of the country's black population.

Thus, Los Van Van's version of identity attempts to bridge the divisions among Cubans. But every gesture of inclusion is simultaneously one of exclusion. And among those excluded are Cubans who do not identify with African traditions. The fact that "Somos cubanos" misquotes verses from "La canción del bongó" (1931) by Cuba's best-known twentieth-century poet, Nicolás Guillén, is relevant to the analysis of the limits that Los Van Van place on their conceptualization of nationality. Near the end of the recording, Rivera sings: "As Nicolás said / Here the finest [person] / Answers as I do."

Guillén's poem presents all Cubans, regardless of race or cultural identification, as participants in an identity deeply imprinted by Africa:

> Brown skin or brown soul
> more from blood than sun,
> those who are not night outside
> get darker deep within.

Here he who is fine
answers if I call!
(Guillén 1952, 12)

In "La canción del bongó," Cubanness is determined by the act of responding to the call of the poetic persona, and in Los Van Van's song, by the manner in which the person responds, but in both texts the emphasis is placed on Afrocentric values that are presented as defining both the poetic call and the hypothetical response of the listener. But for Guillén, Cuban identity is made possible only by forgetting a history of brutality and antagonism between blacks and whites:

in this mulatto land
African and Spanish
—Saint Barbara on one side
on the other, Changó
. . .
it's better to keep quiet
and not raise questions
because we come from far
and we are walking two by two
(Guillén 1952, 13)

Los Van Van, by placing the quotation from Guillén's "Canción del bongó" within the context of the narrative of the negrito, refuse to be silent about the history of exploitation of Cuban blacks. The "finest person" is not only the person who is listening and dancing to Los Van Van's music, but also one who identifies with the cimarrón.

Los Van Van's version of Cuban national identity can be seen as repeating in an Afrocentric key one of the central characteristics of earlier Latin American reflections on national and regional identity. If for Hispanocentric thinkers like José Vasconcelos the celebration of miscegenation concludes in the identification of Latin Americans with Spaniards,[9] Los Van Van's narrative of nationality in "Somos cubanos" ends by blurring the lines between Cuban and black identity. After all, by presenting Cuban identity as being based exclusively on a narrative of black struggle, the difference between Cuban identity and that of other diasporic, arguably even African, blacks is elided. In fact, Los Van Van in earlier songs, such as 1997's "Te pone la cabeza mala," have explicitly celebrated a pan-diasporic black identity.

The last song on *Llegó Van Van/Van Van Is Here* is "Havana City"—sung partially in Spanglish—and addressed to a hypothetical visitor to the Cuban capital. If *Llegó Van Van/Van Van Is Here* begins by implying emigration, it concludes with a song that refers to travel from the United States to Cuba; if it begins by celebrating Afro-Cuban culture, it ends by acknowledging the influence of English and the United States on Cuba. But this reconciliation of the spaces of Cuba—that is, the island and the United States—is grounded on an Afrocentric reinterpretation of the discourse of mestizaje.

CHAPTER EIGHT

Richard Rodriguez in "Borderland"

The Relocation of the Discourse of Mestizaje

The publication of *Days of Obligation: An Argument with My Mexican Father* in 1992 marked a moment of change in the reception of Richard Rodriguez's writings.[1] Rodriguez, once one of the preferred minority voices of the North American right, was suddenly accepted into the fold by a significant number of Chicano critics. In fact, one prominent Chicano intellectual, José David Saldívar, even found proof in Rodriguez's second book that he had converted to the "Mexican point of view" (Saldívar 1997, 50).[2] Paradoxically, *Days of Obligation,* written by a Mexican American opponent of Chicanismo and multiculturalism, a bilingual debunker of bilingual education, a minority critical of affirmative action, has been discovered by some to be a paradigmatic example of a new literature of the border.

This new interpretation of Rodriguez's work has not been unchallenged. For many Chicano—and other—critics Rodriguez's basic positions have not changed. They point out with justification that he still criticizes affirmative action, still opposes bilingual education, and consistently manifests his distrust of multiculturalism and the notion of ethnic identity on which it is generally founded. They read *Days of Obligation* as proof of Rodriguez's unchanged conservative political positions. Rodriguez's critics, however, omit any reference to his opposition to anti-immigrant measures, particularly in his home state of California, or to his continuous defense of gay rights.[3]

Any evaluation of Rodriguez must, therefore, take into account the impossibility of fitting him into any political pigeonhole. If before the publication of *Days of Obligation,* one could describe him as a Mexican American neoconservative, his later essays contradict this characterization. But it is equally difficult to describe him as a "born again" liberal or progressive. The question that has to be raised is whether the seeming political ambiguity of Rodriguez's texts originates in a lack of intellectual coherence, or whether, on the contrary, the source of confusion lies in the critical and political categories used to classify a body of work that resists conventional labels.

This chapter not only analyzes the political implications of the evolution of Rodriguez's thought, but also studies the theoretical consequences of the changes in his points of view. For, as I will argue, his intellectual trajectory has led him to positions that resemble those of prominent mainstream Chicano authors and critics. Today, like Gloria Anzaldúa or José David Saldívar, Rodriguez can be classified as a theorist of the borderlands. However, unlike most critics who emphasize the importance of the border experience—that is, of the continuous interaction between cultures and between ethnic and racial groups—Rodriguez finds in the current emphasis on hybridity a theoretical justification for his ongoing criticism of liberal policies such as bilingual education and affirmative action. His essays, in particular those published after his first autobiographical text, *Hunger of Memory: The Education of Richard Rodriguez* (1982), raise questions about the association made by Chicano intellectuals between the celebration of the borderlands and progressive public policy. *Days of Obligation* and all of Rodriguez's recent writings thus can be seen not only as a contribution to the description and analysis of the border experience, but also as a challenge to the linkage frequently made between the celebration of hybridity and multicultural proposals. But since Rodriguez's approach to the borderlands is based on an updating of the discourse of mestizaje, his writings provide an additional example of the plasticity of this discourse and its continuing use as a basis on which to build national and group identities in both Latin America and the United States.

The Opposition of the Public and the Private

Rodriguez's first book, *Hunger of Memory* (1982), has justly been considered a frontal attack on bilingual education and affirmative action policies. Underlying both Rodriguez's criticism of public policies and the narrative of his life presented in his autobiography is the establishment of an antinomy between the notions of the private and the public. His personal story is narrated as a journey from the private to the public pole of this opposition. And he aligns with the private all of those traits (culture, language, ethnicity, race, and, implicitly, gender and sexual preference) that differentiate one individual from another. The result of his life trajectory is, as he states in his first book, the transformation of Richard Rodriguez from a culturally Mexican and monolingual Spanish-speaking boy into "a middle-class American man" (Rodriguez 1982, 3).

In *Hunger of Memory,* Rodriguez's criticism of bilingual education is rooted in this dichotomy of the private and the public. Spanish is, for him, the private language, the language of the family, of emotion, and of childhood. English, on the other hand, is the public language of society, of education, and of power. Mastery of the latter is opposed to fluency in the former, an opposition based in his own experience: "As I grew fluent in English, I no longer could speak Spanish with confidence" (p. 28). Although Rodriguez qualifies his belief in the validity of this dichotomy by stating that he "wrongly imagined that English was intrinsically a public language and Spanish an intrinsically private one," this binary opposition still underlies his arguments against bilingual education (p. 20). Because it is necessary for children to master the public language, bilingual education is detrimental to their development as public persons.

One must keep in mind that for Rodriguez the elimination of the private sphere is not limited to language, however. Language in *Hunger of Memory* synecdochically stands in for culture and gender.[4] Rodriguez's text extends his conclusions about language to the analysis of culture and gender. For Rodriguez, "one cannot become a public person while still remaining a private one" (p. 34). The participation of an individual in the public sphere implies the erasure of her or his private and personal traits. "One cannot become a public person" without concealing all of one's differentiating traits—ethnicity, culture, and sexuality, as well as language. (The rigidity of the public/private dichotomy in *Hunger of Memory* is underscored by the fact that Rodriguez's defense of a neutral U.S. middle-class identity—that is, his participation in the public arena—is rooted in those private experiences that mark him as different from all other members of the middle class.)

The Blurring of the Public and the Private

The elimination of this binary view of identity is the central modification found in Rodriguez's recent writings. The analysis of language in *Days of Obligation: An Argument with My Mexican Father* (1992) can serve as an example of the manner in which the opposition between the private and the public is replaced by a vision that emphasizes the blurring of the difference between these two fields. Rodriguez notes the intrusion of the private sphere, represented by the Spanish informal second person pronoun *tú,* into the language and culture of the United States: "Mexicans have slipped America a darker beer, a cuisine of *tú.* . . . Mexicans have forced Southwestern Americans to speak Spanish whenever they want their eggs fried or their roses pruned. Mexicans have overwhelmed the Church—eleven o'clock masses in most Valley towns are Spanish masses. By force of numbers, Mexicans have taken over grammar-school classrooms. The Southwest is besotted with the culture of *tú*" (p. 72). Activities and linguistic exchanges belonging to the private sphere—the frying of eggs, the pruning of roses—have a profound impact on the U.S. public sphere. In fact, the church and the school, two public institutions central to Rodriguez's assimilation into the U.S. mainstream—he studied in a Catholic school run by Irish nuns—are now meaningfully described as part of an impure and hybrid public field "besotted with the culture of tú." Moreover, the opposition between the private Mexican and public Anglo cultures, and the corresponding Spanish and English languages, has disappeared. Both Mexicans and Anglos are seen as shaping together a new culturally and linguistically hybrid North American Southwest.

In *Days of Obligation,* the culture of the United States is described as dynamic, as being changed as it incorporates other cultures: "To argue for a common culture is not to propose an exclusionary culture or a static culture. The classroom is always adding to the common text, because America is a dynamic society" (p. 170). Instead of presenting, as in *Hunger of Memory,* a vision of the United States as pure but static, Rodriguez now describes a country that changes culturally and linguistically as it incorporates Mexicans (and other groups). In *Days of Obligation,* the private sphere not only has contaminated the public one, but to a great degree, the former determines the latter.

However, in Rodriguez's writings of the 1990s, language and culture are not the only fields where the rigid separation between the private and the public has broken down. He also presents ethnicity and race as participating in the process of change that characterizes his representation of today's United States. Again, it is possible to see in Rodriguez's current emphasis on racial and ethnic change a rejection of the private/public dichotomy present in his earlier writings.

In *Hunger of Memory* (1982), ethnicity and race are markers of difference that hinder but ultimately do not impede Rodriguez's incorporation into the neutral middle class. His dark skin is a source of anxiety while a child (private person). He speaks of feeling "shame and sexual inferiority" because of his swarthiness (1982, 124). However, after he achieves maturity and becomes assimilated into the public middle class, he comes to realize that "my skin, itself, means nothing" (p. 137). Rodriguez writes as if phenotypic differences effectively disappear once he becomes incorporated into the middle class. In a clearly non-ironical passage, he relates how clerks and attendants ascribe his skin color to a suntan: "The registration clerk in London wonders if I have just been to Switzerland. And the man who carries my luggage in New York guesses the Caribbean. My complexion becomes a mark of my leisure" (p. 137). Participation in the public sphere implies not only the abandonment of any heritage language or culture but also the transmutation of race into complexion. It is significant that in this passage Rodriguez presents the elimination of racial difference not only as a goal but also as something already achieved. Awareness of one's ethnic or racial difference is presented as incompatible with participation in the public U.S. middle class.

The contrast with *Days of Obligation* is again obvious. In his second book his skin color means much, as he discovers when he arrives in Mexico City and notices that "each face looks like mine. No one looks at me" (1992, 24). (The contrast between this Mexican indifference regarding his appearance and the curiosity of the probably non-Latino clerks and porters regarding his "complexion" is telling.) Rodriguez claims to experience a society where (in his case) skin color does not matter, an argument which has after all been part of his defense of assimilation, but his visit to Mexico also leads him to assume ethnicity as part of his public person. In *Days of Obligation,* Rodriguez accepts his identity as a Mexican American. He writes about "other Mexican-Americans, middle class like myself" (p. 67). While he still emphasizes the fact that he belongs to the middle class, he now claims to have an additional hyphenated Mexican American identity. The abstract individual has become a concrete person with a specific ethnic and cultural background.

As the preceding quotation shows, Rodriguez's discovery of his ethnicity does not lead him to propose new binary oppositions between minorities and middle-class North Americans. In the same manner that he visualizes contemporary U.S. language and culture as mixed, as changing, as influenced by Spanish and its culture of tú, Rodriguez now sees racial difference as leading not to separation, but to a new biological hybridity. This modification in Rodriguez's view of the world is linked directly to his experience of Mexico. In *Days of Obligation,* he finds in Mexican racial history—and reality—a map for the changes he sees taking place in the United States: "Mexico initiated the task of the twenty-first century—the renewal of the old, the known world through miscegenation" (p. 25). Miscegenation is of importance not only to an understanding of Mexican society and history, but also to the comprehension of contemporary trends in the United States and the world. In his television essay "The Browning of America" (1998a), Rodriguez makes clear the importance of miscegenation as a force shaping a new United States: "Brown is moving West to East, South to North. Brown terrifies the skinhead in Colorado, bewilders the African-American historian" (1998a). The binary white-nonwhite opposition is replaced in Rodriguez's later essays by an emphasis on a growing "brown" or mestizo reality that is changing the racial and ethnic landscape of the United States as it makes previous oppositions based on race obsolete.

Rodriguez's emphasis on miscegenation as a force changing U.S. identity aligns his recent writings with the Latin American discourse of mestizaje. In fact, Rodriguez's experience of Mexico is linked to his simultaneous coming to grips with what could be called the Mexican intellectual tradition. It is, therefore, possible to see in Rodriguez's essays—beginning with *Days of Obligation*—the surprising application of the Latin American discourse of mestizaje to the analysis of the problems facing the United States today.

The Relocation of the Cosmic Race to the United States

Rodriguez has always been aware of Spanish-language authors. In *Hunger of Memory,* he claims to read "García Lorca and García Márquez"

(1982, 5). More relevant to this analysis, he is on record as having described his autobiography, somewhat inaccurately, as "another *Labyrinth of Solitude*"—referring to Octavio Paz's influential study of Mexican identity (Stavans 1993, 21).[5] What is new in Rodriguez's writings of the 1990s is the discovery of José Vasconcelos's concept of the cosmic race and of the discursive tradition of mestizaje of which Vasconcelos is a significant (though eccentric) representative. In fact, Rodriguez on occasion has even been presented in the public media—it is tempting to assume with his consent—as an "intellectual and spiritual heir of Vasconcelos's" (Rodriguez 1993, 14).

Rodriguez acknowledges the importance of Vasconcelos's thought to his interpretation of Mexico in *Days of Obligation:* "In New England the European and the Indian drew apart to regard each other with suspicion over centuries. Miscegenation was a sin against Protestant individualism. In Mexico the European and the Indian consorted. The ravishment of fabulous Tenochtitlán ended in a marriage of blood—a cosmic race, the Mexican philosopher José Vasconcelos has called it" (1992, 13). Because Mexico has experienced a process of cultural and racial mixture, it prefigures a contemporary United States characterized by a profusion of cultures, languages, and races. Therefore, Rodriguez finds in the cosmic race the necessary conceptual framework with which to understand not only Mexico but also today's changing United States.

This discovery of Vasconcelos is a paradoxical gesture for a critic of Chicanismo. As is well known, the Mexican author has long been one of the central sources of Chicano discourse. An analysis of Rodriguez's relationship with Vasconcelos becomes necessary in order to discern the points of contact and of difference between this Mexican American critic and the (heterogeneous) Chicano mainstream.

Vasconcelos's 1925 book *The Cosmic Race* is a utopian extension of the discourse of mestizaje. Where the discourse of mestizaje generally saw the foundation of the nation, Vasconcelos discovered the beginning of a process of miscegenation that would lead to a postnational and even postracial utopia: "In Spanish America, Nature will no longer repeat one of her partial attempts. This time, the race that will come out of the forgotten Atlantis,[6] will no longer be a race of a single color or of particular features. The future race will not be a fifth, or a sixth race, destined to prevail over its ancestors. What is going to emerge out there is the definitive race, the synthetical race, the integral race, made up of the genius and the blood of all peoples and, for that reason, more capable of true brother-hood and of a truly universal vision" (Vasconcelos 1997, 20). As the pre-ceding quotation makes clear, racial difference is to be superseded by a new kind of racial synthesis that leads to "true brotherhood," and national difference is to be replaced by "universal vision."

In one of his many contradictions, Vasconcelos bases his utopian and universal vision on a profound sense of Latin American nationalism. The original subtitle of his book is, after all, "The Mission of the Ibero-American Race." For Vasconcelos, the cosmic race is an extension of the Ibero–Latin American race as it assimilates ever more racial groups. Therefore, Latin America is the privileged location where the utopian cosmic race will develop and flourish. Moreover, Vasconcelos argues that Latin America is superior to the United States based on the region's supposedly greater capacity for incorporating diverse racial groups.[7]

Rodriguez's vision of the "browning of America" is basically the relocation of the notion of the cosmic race to the United States of the 1990s. Despite the fact that, as we have seen, Rodriguez identifies the cosmic race with the Mexican population—for Vasconcelos, Mexicans and Latin Americans were only the harbingers of what was to come—both au-thors believe generalized miscegenation provides the possibility of elimi-nating social contradictions. For instance, according to Rodriguez, the opposition between Mexican Americans and Anglos is bound to disappear as miscegenation blurs ethnic and racial differences: "The irony is that Latinos as a political force will diminish as the United States becomes more culturally Latin American. Precisely as California becomes more Mexican (more mestizo), a distinct Latino political agenda will become impossible to sustain because we Californians will be too mixed, too inter-married to entertain separate racial/ethnic identities" (1998b, 1). The cos-mic race permits Rodriguez to leave race and ethnicity behind. If all are—or will become—mestizo, then these categories are slowly losing validity. And as this quotation makes clear, miscegenation is linked in Rodriguez's writings to culture. Both culture and race are seen as becoming progres-sively more mixed.

There are some significant differences between Vasconcelos's and Rodriguez's versions of the cosmic race, however. One difference has already been mentioned: Rodriguez sees the United States, rather than Latin America, as being the privileged location for global miscegenation. But Rodriguez's divergences from Vasconcelos run deeper than the mere geographical relocation of the setting for the development of the cosmic race. It can, in fact, be argued that Rodriguez subverts significant aspects of *The Cosmic Race*.

Underlying Vasconcelos's *The Cosmic Race* is a Hispanist and even racialist vision of Latin American history. For Vasconcelos (1997, 17), it is the Spaniards who out of "abundance of love" began the process of miscegenation that will lead to the cosmic race. Moreover, he not only identifies the Latin American population with Spain, but also promotes this identification as an element necessary to the development of the region: "We shall not be great as long as the Spaniard from America does not feel as much a Spaniard as the sons of Spain" (p. 11). In fact, despite his consistent celebration of miscegenation, Vasconcelos's references to Amerindians, blacks, and Asians reflect racialist classifications and stereotypes.[8]

Rodriguez does not share Vasconcelos's Hispanophilia. On the contrary, in *Days of Obligation* (and in other recent essays), it is the openness of the Amerindians to the new, their curiosity—whether expressed in sexual desire for the European colonizers or in the appropriation of European culture, language, and religion—that explains the mestizo culture and population of Mexico. In fact, for Rodriguez the Amerindian absorbs the European through miscegenation. In his version of the archetypal story of Mexican mestizaje, Malinche, Cortes's translator and lover, is "the seducer of Spain," an active, not a passive, participant (Rodriguez 1992, 22).[9] This desire for the new explains why what was once foreign to the Amerindian and central to the identity of the Spaniards, such as their language or religion, is appropriated by the Amerindians. As Rodriguez points out, "Catholicism has become an Indian religion" and "Spanish is now an Indian language" (pp. 20, 24). Therefore, it should surprise no one that Rodriguez, the foremost contemporary Mexican American defender of assimilation, identifies strongly with the Amerindian. In *Days of Obligation* he states, "I take it as an Indian achievement that I am alive, that I am Catholic, that I speak English, that I am an American. My life began, it did not end, in the sixteenth century" (p. 24).[10]

But Rodriguez does not limit the association of Amerindians with assimilation to a distant historical past. He identifies them with the Mexican and Central American population, and discovers that they are still assimilating and appropriating modernity: "The Indian has chosen to survive, to consort with the living, to live in the city, to crawl on her hands and knees, if need be, to Mexico City" (p. 24). But Amerindians are not only migrating to Mexico City, they are also coming to the United States: "most of the illegal immigrants, those teenagers who will make a run for it tonight from Tijuana to San Diego, are Indians. We call them Guatemalans or Mexicans, but they are Indians" (1995d, 1). While Vasconcelos argues that the Spanish legacy is what is leading the "Spaniard from America" to continue incorporating other ethnic groups (biologically and culturally), Rodriguez believes that it is the Amerindian who is the prototype of the new brown/mestizo race being created in the United States by the miscegenation of the different ethnic and racial groups living in the country.

Femininity, Agency, and Curiosity in Mestizaje

In Vasconcelos's writings, beginning with the Spanish conquistadors who chose their mates from among the conquered people, the cosmic race is implicitly the creation of the male.[11] Again Rodriguez differs from his predecessor. Rodriguez, as can be seen from the reference to Malinche, identifies the Amerindian with the female. While Amerindians have frequently been coded as female in the discourse of mestizaje, Rodriguez rejects the negative stereotypes absurdly associated with women through his emphasis on Amerindian and female agency. As he indicates in *Days of Obligation,* "I assure you Mexico has an Indian point of view as well, a female point of view" (1992, 22). In his writings, femininity is no longer associated with passivity or silence.

Rodriguez's vision of the Amerindian as female is directly linked to his attempt at eliminating ethnic, racial, and national binary oppositions: "The Indian stands in the same relationship to modernity as she did to Spain—willing to marry, to breed, to disappear in order to ensure her inclusion in time" (p. 24). Implicit in this image of the Amerindian as female is the notion of incorporation. The Amerindian, in Rodriguez's historical narrative and social analysis, is characterized by an "absorbent strength" that is clearly defined as female (p. 20). Again, Rodriguez's identification with the Amerindian, understood as representing a female principle, contrasts with his self-description in *Hunger of Memory* as a "middle-class American man." For, as we will see, this earlier self-definition implies more than the obvious fact that Rodriguez is a man.

Rodriguez has implicitly criticized his own *Hunger of Memory* by describing the binary logic characteristic of his autobiography as "masculine." During an interview with Paul Crowley, as part of his explanation about his own identification with the Amerindian, Rodriguez notes that, "There may be a feminine impulse within colonial history that we do not understand. It's not as simple as two males butting heads—one wins, the other loses. Perhaps there is such a thing as seduction. Conversion. Perhaps cultures absorb one another. If it is true that the Franciscan padre forced the Eucharist down the Indian's throat, maybe she forgot to close her mouth. Maybe she swallowed the Franciscan priest" (1995c, 8). Rodriguez's writings can, therefore, be described as moving from a "masculine" perspective—the butting heads of the either-or opposition between the Chicano and the Anglo found in *Hunger of Memory*—to what he defines as a feminine and Indian perspective. Beginning with *Days of Obligation,* Rodriguez finds in hybridity the means to go beyond cultural, racial, and ethnic oppositions. Femininity becomes therefore synonymous with this obsolescence of cultural and racial oppositions. For instance, one can see in the interview passage quoted previously a clear representation of the manner in which Rodriguez eliminates binary oppositions from his historical and cultural analyses. In this text, the Amerindian/female's experiences of catechization and acculturation are described as neither the simple loss of indigenous culture nor the exclusive appropriation of the foreign culture for the individual's own benefit. The Eucharist is both swallowed and forced down the throat. The loss of culture is also the gain of culture. Seduction is synonymous with conversion. Assimilation implies the appropriation of culture. Therefore, according to Rodriguez, Amerindians are female in that they assimilate Spanish culture and simultaneously change the culture they receive from the conquistadors. (But Rodriguez's consistent breaking down of binary oppositions in his analyses leads him to de-emphasize real-life historical contradictions. As we have seen in his writings, the genocide and exploitation of the Amerindian that began with the conquest of Mexico becomes a positive cultural absorption and, at his most explicit, a Lorcan "marriage of blood" [pp. 74, 169].)

The links between the female and Mexico are obvious. For Mexico is described as the country of the Indian—marked as female in Rodriguez's writings—and as the land of the cosmic race that is also breaking down binary oppositions. It should not surprise anyone that he associates Mexico with motherhood. He writes about "mother Mexico" and "the maternity of Mexico" (1992, 65, 72).[12] For Rodriguez, miscegenation, the decision to embrace the racial/cultural other instead of "butting heads," is the ulti-mate manifestation of the "female impulse."

This female desire for the other, this curiosity, this capacity to break down oppositions, is, however, not exclusive to women. After all, men can desire the other or appropriate and assimilate into foreign cultures. Therefore, in addition to Malinche, whom Rodriguez has claimed as his "grandmother" (1995c, 8), the character that exemplifies the cultural and sexual curiosity of the Indian is Caliban.

Caliban is mentioned in both *Hunger of Memory* and *Days of Obliga-tion*. In fact, *Hunger of Memory* begins with a reference to Shakespeare's archetypal Indian. There, Rodriguez surprisingly identifies with Caliban: "I have taken Caliban's advice. I have stolen their books. I will have some run of this isle" (1982, 3). The element of paradox present in Rodriguez's paean to assimilation beginning with this reference to Caliban, the ran-corous Amerindian, is undeniable.[13] Rodriguez's autobiography is not, after all, a text on learning to curse the European. However, the "male butting of heads" is present not only in the rigid opposition between middle-class Americans and Chicanos (or any other minority group) cen-tral to this autobiographical narrative, but also in the manner in which the figure of Caliban is introduced in the text. Although Caliban's implicit opposition to the middle-class U.S. Prospero is defused throughout the rest of the text, Rodriguez, in this quotation, presents his own relationship with Anglo culture as an act of theft and, therefore, as an act of aggression.

Days of Obligation, on the other hand, describes Caliban's attitude toward Prospero in different terms: "Shakespeare saw Caliban eyeing his master's books—well, why not his master as well" (1992, 23). While both of Rodriguez's books emphasize Caliban's desire for Prospero's culture, the context is different. Here the relationship between Caliban and Anglo culture, and now also Anglo people, is presented as an additional example of the Amerindian's desire for the other and the other's culture (books) that underlies Rodriguez's appropriation of the notion of the cosmic race. *Hunger of Memory,* therefore, presents a masculine version of intercultural contact where assimilation is paradoxically an act of aggression. *Days of Obligation,* on the contrary, links sexual and cultural desire in a manner consistent with Rodriguez's vision of female agency as exemplified by Malinche and Amerindians in general.

It is tempting to link Rodriguez's discovery of Mexico, of Vascon-celos, and of the Indian not only to his visits to Mexico, but to a second personal experience that, as Saldívar points out, is also central to an under-standing of *Days of Obligation:* Rodriguez's coming out as a gay man (Saldívar 1997, 149–50). For Rodriguez's coding of Mexico and the Indian as female—but not passive—seems to link his ethnic and his sexual "com-ings out." *Days of Obligation* is not only a record of Rodriguez's discovery of Mexico. It also presents Rodriguez's oblique, somewhat ambiguous, but still significant acceptance of his homosexuality.[14] In Rodriguez's second book, his analyses of gender, race, and ethnicity are, as we have seen, interrelated. One must remember, however, that his association of the Indian with femininity is not the establishment of a rigid male-female dichotomy, but part of a vision of the Indian/female as dissolving di-chotomies including that of the male and female. His own coming out as gay can be seen, therefore, as compatible with the breakdown of binary oppositions that characterizes his later writings.

Immigration and the Border Experience

Underlying Rodriguez's recent discovery of hybridity is an emphasis on the border experience. While *Hunger of Memory,* being the autobiography of a child of Mexican parents living in the United States, could not avoid dealing with immigration, this topic is consigned to a personal prehistory. Rodriguez has become "a middle-class American man"; his parents are the immigrants. But beginning with *Days of Obligation,* immigration and the border experience become central in Rodriguez's essays. Not only are immigrants slipping the United States the culture of tú and helping to form a new mestizo race, but in addition the Mexican American border experience becomes the prism through which the author sees and analyses current U.S. and world reality. Intercultural and interracial contact in today's United States, Rodriguez's current main concern, is taking place not through conquest, as was the case in Mexico, but through migration. This new emphasis on migration and the key position it occupies in his cultural analyses bears an uncanny similarity to the writings of the new Chicano theorists of the borderlands and of the border.

As is well known, "border" and "borderlands" are generally used interchangeably by literary scholars despite their having separate, though related, histories. In fact, the concept of the Spanish borderlands, or sim-ply the borderlands, has long been in use in the historiography of Spanish America in the United States and in literary studies. Coined in the 1920s to refer to "that area of the continental United States that had been part of the once expansive Spanish Empire in the New World" (Driscoll 1993, 8),[15] the notion of the borderlands was applied by its originator, Herbert Bolton, to the field of literary studies. For instance, he wrote of a "literature of the borderlands" that included both historical and fictional narratives set in the area, and that had as its most famous exemplar Helen Hunt Jackson's 1884 novel *Ramona* (Driscoll 1993, 13).[16]

The concept of the border has its own independent, though related, history. Border studies, as an autonomous discipline, was founded in the 1950s by social scientists Julián Samora, Gilbert Cárdenas, and, in particular, Charles Loomis. The works of these scholars were mostly anthropological and sociological in bent, dealing with topics such as "interethnic relations in two southwestern high schools" or "folk medicine in the Southwest" (Driscoll 1993, 23, 31). Despite its origins in the social sciences, the discipline of border studies soon incorporated the historical and literary themes previously associated with the concept of the borderlands. It could be argued that this incorporation of the topics linked with the borderlands into border studies is implicit in the definitions of these concepts. Both the borderlands and the border were generally seen as unproblematic denotations of concrete geographical areas. One can map the borderlands;[17] and as recently as 1993 a border scholar could describe the subject matter of her discipline as a "straightforward and self evident concept," and geographically define the border as the region surrounding the actual boundary between the United States and Mexico "whose identity, economic activities, cultural life, etc., supersedes its binational stature to be integrated in many respects" (Driscoll 1993, 3). What once was the borderlands became the border.

Recent theories of the borderlands and of the border have significantly altered the former mainstream use of these concepts.[18] These signifiers, which once referred to clearly identifiable signifieds are now described in highly abstract terms. Gloria Anzaldúa's *Borderlands/La Frontera* (1987), arguably the foundational text of these new interpretations of the border/borderlands, no longer refers to a mapped or "mappable" area.[19] While still related to the boundary between Mexico and the United States, the borderlands are now described as a "vague and undetermined place created by the emotional residue of an unnatural boundary" (Anzaldúa 1987, 3). Saldívar, a more concrete thinker than Anzaldúa, still writes about "an emerging U.S.–Mexico *frontera* imagi-

nary" that is helping to "undo the militarized frontier 'field-Imaginary' "
(Saldívar 1997, xii). Both Anzaldúa and Saldívar reconfigure earlier conceptualizations of the borderlands and the border by discovering in the
fluid hybridity characteristic of the area's population and their culture a
paradigm with which to interpret the United States and the world.[20]

This new Chicano border/borderlands theory—and its concomitant
celebration of a hybrid identity—implies a significant change from the
versions of identity proposed during the heyday of the Chicano Movement in the 1960s and 1970s. As Saldívar (1997, 116) notes, earlier versions
of Chicano identity were "separatist in nature," and thus conceptualized
Chicanismo by and through an opposition to mainstream U.S. society. In
fact, a surprising parallel can be made between the evolution of Rodriguez's writings and this variant of Chicano thought. If, on the one hand,
Rodriguez once described his "middle-class American" identity as being
built on an opposition to Mexican (and Mexican American) cultural traits,
Chicanos, on the other hand, based their identity on their opposition to
and separation from the mainstream United States. Underlying both versions of identity were dichotomies between U.S. and Chicano identities.
Rodriguez and Chicanos differed on which pole they chose to privilege
and which to denigrate. However, Rodriguez and (many) mainstream
Chicano authors have evolved toward a celebration of hybridity and the
border.

The central difference between Chicano theories of the borderlands
and Rodriguez's writings lies neither in their privileging of the border and
immigrant experience nor in their celebration of hybridity. What separates Rodriguez from this new Chicano mainstream is that theorists of the
border generally see hybridity as leading to a progressively greater heterogeneity. For instance, although Anzaldúa (1987, 77) writes about the "new
mestiza" and claims Vasconcelos as an important precursor of contemporary Chicano theorists, she differs from her Mexican predecessor in not
describing this new mestizaje as leading to the creation of a homogeneous
new race and culture.[21] According to Anzaldúa, the new mestiza is the
inhabitant of a space between cultures, nationalities, and genders, capable
of being one and all things, of belonging to all cultural backgrounds:
"[She] learns to be an Indian in Mexican culture, to be Mexican from an
Anglo point of view. She learns to juggle cultures. She has a plural personality, she operates in a pluralistic mode—nothing is thrust out, the good,
the bad, and the ugly, nothing rejected, nothing abandoned. Not only does

she sustain contradictions, she turns the ambivalence into something else" (p. 79). While Rodriguez's analysis discovers a process of miscegenation and cultural interaction that is developing a mestizo and homogeneous United States, Anzaldúa refuses to see intercultural (and interracial) contact as leading to a new homogeneity. Her concept of the mestiza consciousness is imagined as the internalization of the contradictions between cultures (p. 77). Therefore, her new mestiza is not the equivalent of Rodriguez's brown American. Instead of Rodriguez's modified, expanded, mestizo, but ultimately homogeneous U.S. identity, Anzaldúa sees the future as characterized by the proliferation of bicultural and multicultural identities. While she mentions mestizaje, the emphasis is not on the creation of a new race or culture but, rather, on the development of a new heterogeneous consciousness. The new mestiza is, therefore, not necessarily a multiracial or postracial individual; she is just one able and willing to live in more than one culture at a time. The celebration of the border, therefore, implies the simultaneous celebration of hybridity and of the permanence of cultural difference. In Anzaldúa's analysis, hybridization breeds even more heterogeneity. Rodriguez, on the other hand, envisions a developing hybrid homogeneity.[22]

Rodriguez's writings conclude in a vision of the future of the United States where racial and cultural differences disappear. He is not, however, proposing a new version of the melting pot, if we understand this concept as a process of eliminating all cultural differences and imposing a new Anglo identity on minority individuals. On the contrary, Rodriguez believes that miscegenation and intercultural contact are giving rise to a new, brown U.S. reality that will finally make real the promises of equality of opportunity and the dreams of cultural inclusiveness that have frequently characterized this country. As we have seen, this vision of the future implies at its core a direct appropriation of the notion of the cosmic race and of the discourse of mestizaje. Saldívar (1997, 151), therefore, is correct when he writes about Rodriguez that his vision of "the future of California is its Latinoization." (And one could add that California, for Rodriguez, is at the vanguard of a process that is changing the United States as a whole.)

But one of the challenges that Rodriguez's writings present for current Chicano theorists of the border rests on what is meant by Latinoization. While both Saldívar and Rodriguez define (and celebrate) Latinoization as leading to a fluid and interconnected relationship between North and South, between Mexico and the United States, this is not all it means for Rodriguez. For him, Latinoization is also a process that leads to the creation of a new racially and culturally mestizo United States. He, in fact, sees Latin America as the paradigmatic example of a society originally constituted by an ethnically, racially, and culturally heterogeneous population that has been (at least partially) capable of reconciling this diversity and subsuming it under a new homogeneous identity. While his celebration of intercultural connections and hybridity echoes that of Chicano theorists of the border—and is a sign that Rodriguez participates in contemporary critical paradigms—his analysis reaches conclusions that contradict those of other Chicano critics. Rodriguez's writings, therefore, question the automatic linkage made by critics such as Saldívar or Anzaldúa between an emphasis on hybridity and multiculturalism.

Moreover, Rodriguez's "Mexican point of view" undermines any attempt to classify him politically. His analysis of Mexican and border hybridity leads him simultaneously to hold positions associated with both the political right and the left. In fact, Rodriguez is now able to present his points of view as more Mexican than those of the Chicano mainstream. As he writes, criticizing one of the central tenets of contemporary Chicano politics and thought, "Mexico has no notion of multiculturalism" (1998b, 1). He now bases his criticisms of liberal policies not on the binary opposition between public and private spheres, but on his celebration of the cosmic race. This appropriation of the cosmic race permits him to theorize the obsolescence of the concept of race itself. According to Rodriguez, affirmative action becomes unnecessary because racial and cultural difference—on which this policy is based—is shown to be disappearing. He similarly sees U.S. cultural diversity as leading to a new brown homogeneity. By going beyond the binary oppositions that characterized *Hunger of Memory,* Rodriguez has abandoned the strident hostility toward liberal programs present in his earlier writings.[23] However, he has also undermined the justification for these same programs. But the same emphasis on hybridity also structures his opposition to anti-immigrant measures and his defense of gay rights.

As we have seen, the essays of Richard Rodriguez raise central theoretical and political questions for the Chicano and Mexican American community. On the one hand, he problematizes the characterization of what constitutes contemporary Chicano/Mexican American discourse. If the celebration of the border and hybridity is central to one's definition of

Chicanismo, there is no doubt that Rodriguez has to be considered a representative Mexican American author. On the other hand, if the defense of cultural difference is what is deemed significant, Rodriguez is clearly a heretical voice. But Rodriguez's writings also question notions of what is progressive or conservative within the Chicano/Mexican American community. Is he conservative because of his opposition to multiculturalism (as a policy), bilingual education, and affirmative action? Or, on the contrary, should he be considered a radical defender of immigrant and gay rights?

Regardless of how one answers these questions, they serve as proof of the importance of Rodriguez within contemporary Chicano and Mexican American writing and thought. His essays challenge established definitions of what it means to be a Mexican American. His writings bear an uncanny similarity—in the sense of being both strange and familiar—to the writings of the Chicano mainstream. Rodriguez's intellectual forays into the borderlands show us some of the possibilities hidden within mainstream Chicano thought. Therefore, his writings offer a possible starting point for a re-evaluation of Chicano identity and discourse. But they also serve as a clear example of the manner in which the Latin American discourse of mestizaje can be translated into a new cultural context and used to ground discussion of some of the most characteristic and pressing problems of our time.

CHAPTER NINE

From Mestizaje to Multiculturalism

On José María Arguedas, New Mestizas, Demons, and the Uncanny

Probably no Latin American author faced more fully in his life and work the questions implicit in the discourse of mestizaje than did the Peruvian novelist and anthropologist José María Arguedas (1911–1969). Born in the Peruvian Andes and raised in intimate contact with the Quechua communities, he produced literary and anthropological works dealing exclusively with the possibility of creating a new Peruvian identity that would heal the ethnic, linguistic, and cultural rift that has characterized the country since the conquest. The majority of his novels and short stories imply a radical version of the discourse of mestizaje that attempts to create a truly hybrid nationality that incorporates "into the current of wisdom and art of the Peruvian criollo that other stream of flow of art and wisdom" of the Amerindian cultures (Arguedas 2000, 268). Despite the fact that his novels, in particular *Deep Rivers* (1958), radicalize the notion of mestizaje to the point where this text has been seen as the principal example of regional transculturation, the preceding statement presents his work as enriching and modifying but not necessarily supplanting the national mainstream.[1] However, in his posthumous novel, *The Fox from Up Above and the Fox from Down Below,* originally published in 1971, some passages, such as that quoted previously, repeat a more conventional version of the discourse of mestizaje whereas others anticipate current postmodern and multicultural discussions on identity taking place in the United States and Western Europe.

Set in the fishing boomtown of Chimbote, *The Fox from Up Above and the Fox from Down Below* is composed of alternating fictional and diary sections, the latter dealing with Arguedas's struggle with his suicidal tendencies. It also includes Arguedas's acceptance speech for the 1968 Inca Garcilaso Award, titled "I Am Not an Acculturated Man." In sections of this text, Arguedas goes beyond mainstream versions of the discourse of mestizaje. Here Arguedas celebrates a radical biculturalism as the basis of Peruvian identity. He defiantly declares, "I am not an acculturated man; I am a Peruvian who, like a cheerful demon, proudly speaks in Christian and in Indian, in Spanish and in Quechua" (Arguedas 2000, 257). In this passage, Arguedas leaves behind conventional versions of mestizaje as the basis of identity. He defines his Peruvian identity as based not only on Quechua-Spanish bilingualism, but also on full participation in both indigenous and criollo cultures and, therefore, on the fact and possibility of being Indian and criollo. He is aware of how innovative this version of national identity must have seemed at the time. Presenting himself as a paradigmatic example, Arguedas describes this new bicultural Peruvian as a "cheerful demon." The figure of the cheerful demon—obviously related to that of the trickster—denies binary oppositions and systems of classification based on them. In other words, Arguedas presents his new version of what constitutes the basis of Peruvian identity not only as contradicting any dichotomy based on the opposition between Spanish and Quechua, or criollo and Indian, but also as being outside traditional conceptualizations of nationality or identity.

It is tempting to see in Arguedas's cheerful demon an earlier analogue to Gloria Anzaldúa's new mestiza. Anzaldúa describes the new mestiza as also voiding binary oppositions. In a passage partially quoted in the previous chapter, Anzaldúa (1997, 151) makes this clear: "The new mestiza copes by developing a tolerance for contradictions, a tolerance for ambiguity. She learns to be an Indian in Mexican culture, to be a Mexican from an Anglo point of view. She learns to juggle cultures. She has a plural personality, she operates in a pluralistic mode—nothing is thrust out, the good, the bad and the ugly, nothing rejected, nothing abandoned." Both the cheerful demon and the new mestiza incorporate cultural plurality and, therefore, deny dichotomies such as those between the Mexican and Anglo (in Anzaldúa's case) or Amerindian and criollo (in Arguedas's) that have been at the core of attempts to construct identity in Peru and the North American Southwest. But Arguedas's and Anzaldúa's statements have implications that go beyond conventional notions of hybrid identity—such as those founded in cultural or biological mestizaje. Both authors imply that the multicultural realities of contemporary Peru and the North American borderlands lead to the breakdown not only of unitary national or ethnic identities, but also of the monolithic self.

Arguedas further defined and radicalized his vision of a plural Peru in the personal diary entries that are part of *The Fox from Up Above and the Fox from Down Below*. In "Last Diary?," written in 1969 as a kind of public suicide note, he states:

> And that country in which there are all kinds of men and natural environments—I am leaving it while it is boiling with the strengths of so many different essences that are swirling to become transformed at the end of a bloody centuries-old struggle; that struggle has truly begun to break through the shackles and gloomy darkness that have been used to keep them separated and restraining themselves. In me bid farewell to an era of Peru, whose roots will always be sucking juice from the soil to nourish those who live in our homeland, where any man no longer shackled and brutalized by selfishness can joyfully experience all of the homelands. (Arguedas 2000, 259–60)

In this passage, literally Arguedas's last words on the problems of mestizaje in Peru, he goes beyond his statements of less than a year before in "I Am Not an Acculturated Man." Writing at a time when improvements in transportation, rapid population growth, industrial development, and the concomitant expansion in the demand for labor have broken down the formerly rigid geographical and cultural division between the criollo coast and the indigenous Andes, Arguedas describes Peru as not just a bicultural nation but as a multicultural cauldron. The migration of Quechua and Aymara peasants seeking work to the major coastal cities of Lima and Chimbote had by this time turned the country into a true borderland in which the two original groups (Spaniards and Amerindians) had given rise to numerous cultural mixtures that were also influenced by the presence of other migrant communities (black, Chinese, Japanese, etc). Thus in *The Fox from Up Above and the Fox from Down Below*, Arguedas describes the country as a plural, multicultural, and even multinational space. And despite the obvious shadow cast by his imminent suicide, he clearly presents this plural reality in positive terms.

This optimistic interpretation of hybrid reality and future is also characteristic of theories of the borderlands such as Anzaldúa's. For the Chicana critic, "A massive uprooting of dualistic thinking in the individual and collective consciousness is the beginning of a long struggle, but one that could, in our best hopes, bring us to the end of rape, of violence, of war" (Anzaldúa 1987, 80). Like Arguedas, Anzaldúa sees in the breakdown of binary oppositions the precondition for the creation of a utopian reality.

Arguedas's new definition of Peruvian national identity foreshadows not only Anzaldúa's new mestiza, but also other radical postmodern reconceptualizations of identity produced in Western Europe, which has also become a heterogeneous borderland as it receives migrants from the so-called Third World (mainly Africa and the Near East). Julia Kristeva, the well-known Franco-Bulgarian intellectual, describes the changes experienced by her adopted country as "the kaleidoscope that France is becoming—kaleidoscope first of the Mediterranean and progressively of the third world" (Kristeva 1991, 194). She also theorizes the changes in identity appropriate to this new kaleidoscopic French and, by extension, European reality by appealing to psychoanalysis, in particular, the Freudian concept of the uncanny. For Kristeva, a solution to the social and cultural tensions between "natives" (French/Europeans) and "foreigners" can be found by coming to grips with the fact that our relations with foreigners (whoever they may be) are ultimately mediated by our unconscious needs, desires, and fantasies: "To discover our disturbing otherness, for that indeed is what bursts in to confront that 'demon,' that threat, that apprehension generated by the projective apparition of the other at the heart of what we persist in maintaining as a proper, solid 'us.' By recognizing our uncanny strangeness we shall neither suffer from it nor enjoy it from the outside. The foreigner is within me, hence we are all foreigners. If I am a foreigner, there are no foreigners" (p. 192). If foreigners are uncanny, it is precisely because they are both strange and familiar or, better said, exhibit that in ourselves with which we have not come to terms. Foreignness, instead of belonging to the "other," becomes, therefore, a central characteristic of all human beings.

Despite the obvious difference in the level of abstraction, the affinity between Kristeva's analysis (motivated by the existence of a European borderlands) and those of Anzaldúa and Arguedas should be obvious. In all of these cases, there is a denial of the dichotomies on which identity has been built (Anglo-Mexican, criollo-Indian, French-foreign) based on what could be loosely called the identification of otherness within the self. By denying the notion of a seamless individual identity, these authors can be seen as questioning the traditional definition of the nation as based on a unitary or unified race, culture, or language. Therefore, these versions of identity can all be construed as compatible with, if not actual versions of, multiculturalism. There are nevertheless important differences. Both Arguedas and Anzaldúa base their versions of individual and plural identity in concrete historical oppositions between criollo versus Indian and Anglo versus Mexican, respectively, while Kristeva finds otherness in the psychological makeup of every individual, regardless of specific social, cultural, or political realities. For Kristeva, contemporary European cultural heterogeneity presents an opportunity to face up to this defining, though long repressed, human characteristic.

The notion of a culturally plural identity is one of the possibilities that has always been present in the definition of the nation as mestizo—that is, as founded on bi- or multicultural populations. While a new homogeneous hybridity has in Latin America most often been seen as the result of mestizaje, this is not the only possible result of the coexistence of varied cultural, racial, or ethnic groups. The creation of a new multilingual and multicultural individual, population, and nation is an equally valid possibility.

Moreover, Arguedas's writings are proof that the privileging of cultural and linguistic heterogeneity is not incompatible with a belief in the necessity of a national framework. As is clear from the passages quoted previously, *The Fox from Up Above and the Fox from Down Below* is fueled by a passionate patriotism. Thus Arguedas's cheerful demon, rather than denying Peruvian identity, may be seen as resolving the central contradiction of the country's history: the split between a criollo and indigenous Peru. This division not only would be internalized but also healed by the individual's capacity to fully appreciate and participate in both cultural traditions. It is precisely because this experience is seen not only as denying binary oppositions, but also as personally enriching, that Arguedas describes the demon as cheerful. *The Fox from Up Above and the Fox from Down Below* insinuates a vision of Peru based on the equality of Indian and Spanish language and culture that is the utopian core of Arguedas's final writings. In these, the quality of being bi- or multicultural is the definition of Peruvianness, not a threat to the nation.

But the emphasis on a bi- or multicultural present does not necessarily contradict a belief in an ultimate cultural or racial fusion. Recall that one of the criticisms of the discourse of mestizaje has been that it frequently has served as a cover for the acculturation of indigenous groups into Western/criollo culture. By postulating a generalized biculturalism, by defining Peruvianness as the capacity of being cognizant of both criollo and Quechua cultures and their respective languages, Arguedas can also be seen as envisioning a future homogeneity where both Indian and criollo traditions would be in transcultural equilibrium. The quality of being bi- or multicultural thus can be the precondition for a true mestizaje free from the taint of acculturation. Analysts of the heterogeneous and contradictory North American multiculturalism (and its underlying social reality) have also argued that it "may lead to a greater and more profoundly integrated common culture" (Stewart 1999, 54).

But simultaneous with this optimistic interpretation of Peru's multicultural reality and future, we may find in *The Fox from Up Above and the Fox from Down Below* a pessimistic fictional representation of the results of the coming together of Amerindian and criollo populations. Arguedas's novel, which in its fictional sections details the lives of the (mostly Andean) migrants in the industrial fishing port of Chimbote, presents a fresco not of transculturation (which implies creativity and agency), nor of pregnant bi- or multiculturalism, nor even of acculturation (which is, after all, synonymous with the full assimilation into and acceptance of a new culture), but rather of a generalized and apparently permanent deculturation. Thus one of the characters describes life in Chimbote in the following terms: "Here in Chimbote the most of us shanty people has all come out more or less equal these last years; we've all come out equal at bein' the poorest of the poor, which probably appears to be a lot more burdensome here that it's up in the high Andes, because here have gathered together the people forsaken by God and the ones forsaken by the earth, because by now nobodies in the slums of Chimbote is from any parts, or any town" (Arguedas [1971] 1992, 229).[2] In Arguedas's last fiction, the Peruvian borderlands are characterized by loss of culture and language (and therefore identity), and by generalized poverty.

The key to this aspect of Arguedas's contradictory reflections on the Peruvian borderlands can be found in the passage quoted from the "Last Diary?," which refers to selfishness as "shackling" and "brutalizing" Peruvians. This, as should be obvious, is a clear reference to capitalism, to the market that is, in fact, the force bringing together Peruvians of all regions, races, and cultural and linguistic backgrounds. *The Fox from Up Above and the Fox from Down Below* shows that by transforming Andean migrants into poverty-stricken individuals searching paradoxically to maximize their income, capitalism strips them of all significant cultural difference. Arguedas thus struggles with one of the key contradictions of (post) modernity in the periphery: capitalism, while bringing about the exchange and connection that makes an egalitarian mestizaje conceivable, dilutes cultural difference to the point that such mixture loses much of its positive meaning. Cornejo Polar, one of Arguedas's ablest commentators, summarizes this aspect of *The Fox from Up Above and the Fox from Down Below:*

> The ancient and splendid culture of solidarity is destroyed by the imperative of individual competitiveness. In a similar manner, the religious respect for nature is unseated by the capitalistic urgency to exploit resources without limits. Therefore, the Andean migrants, fallen into the machinery of an aberrant modernity, can barely preserve the values of the original world. In other words, verifiable reality affirms the intercommunication [between the Andes and the coast] symbolized by the "foxes,"[3] but confers to it a totally opposite meaning; it is, on the contrary, an occasion of corruption and alienation. It is as if concrete history mocked utopia and myth. (Cornejo Polar 1992, 301)

Arguedas, probably following the lead of José Carlos Mariátegui, incorporates contemporary economic and social Peruvian reality into his final novel and, therefore, brings the problematics of class into his discussion of culture and mestizaje. But unlike Mariátegui, Arguedas is unable to find in the fictional sections of his novel any point of convergence between culture, class, and the possibility of political and social change. For in Arguedas's fictional world, the disruption caused by economic change has led to the dilution of cultural bounds but not to their replacement by class consciousness or solidarity. Thus Arguedas's awareness of the economic changes his country was beginning to experience in the 1960s undermined the optimistic diagnosis of Peruvian hybridity present in the essay and diary sections of the novel.

In the fictional section of Arguedas's novel, the economic impoverishment of the migrants to Chimbote is presented as leading to their cultural impoverishment. To use the term coined by Robert Kurz and transferred by Neil Larsen into literary studies, the Andean migrants have become "monetary subjects without money" (Larsen 1997). That is, they have been incorporated into capitalism in such an extremely marginal position that their participation in the national and international economy as either laborers or consumers is severely limited. Poverty, environmental degradation, and deculturation characterize the urban experience of the dwellers of Chimbote, who are symptomatically described as "forsaken by God and the earth" (Arguedas [1971] 1992, 229). Because they have lost their cultural moorings, Arguedas's migrants have been stripped of any sense of collective identity. One could, therefore, argue that Arguedas's Chimbote not only represents the specific cultural and economic realities of Peru of the late 1960s, but also depicts the reality faced today by a large segment of the world's population who have been or are being incorporated into the national and transnational market economies.

One cannot apply to *The Fox from Up Above and the Fox from Down Below* Larsen's criticism of much postcolonial (and, one could add, postmodern, multicultural, etc.) thought: "Postcolonialism forgets, or never grasps, that the flip-side of 'hybridity,' 'diasporic consciousness,' etc., is the postcatastrophic holocaust of 'monetary subjects without money'" (1997, par. 20). But the price paid by Arguedas for this awareness is contradiction. If on the one hand, he celebrates hybridity as being individually and nationally enriching, and as leading to the elimination of socially and personally repressive dichotomies, on the other he represents, in the fictional sections of the novel, the dilution of all national, linguistic, and ethnic identity as the result of an exploitative and dehumanizing economic reality.

Despite their common optimism and their disregard for problems of class and economics (a fact arguably justified by the First World ground of their reflections) even Kristeva's and Anzaldúa's analyses may be read as implying a similar loss of relevance of cultural difference. After all, if everyone is a new mestiza, then being one is the norm and the basis on which the status quo will be built. In a similar manner, Kristeva's domestication of otherness as a psychological construct may be grounded on the real-life domestication of cultural difference to be found in our contemporary world. As in Anzaldúa's analysis, if all are the other, then otherness is no longer truly significant.[4]

Conclusion

With this brief analysis of Arguedas's final novel concludes this study of some of the many avatars of the discourse of mestizaje, not because I consider Arguedas's novel to constitute an end or conclusion to a discursive tradition that, as we have seen in the chapters on Los Van Van or Richard Rodriguez, is still alive and capable of reinterpretation, but rather because *The Fox from Up Above and the Fox from Down Below* raises questions that frequently have been obscured in past and present celebrations of hybridity, or in the mirror-image jeremiads for the loss of a purity that has never existed. Arguedas, in his contradictions, in his incapacity to be consistently optimistic or critical, cannot help but lead us to ask whether our contemporary world, transformed into a "global village" by multinational capitalism and media, is leading to the psychological enrichment of individuals or if, on the contrary, we may be seeing the progressive cultural, economic, environmental, and moral impoverishment of the majority of the world's population: their transformation into "monetary subjects without money." If Arguedas's fictional Chimbote can be seen as a dystopian representation of our contemporary world borderlands, his optimistic predictions of the results of mestizaje present a utopian parallel to the positive readings of cultural and economic interconnection proposed by those who find in hybridity the way out of our history of intercultural, international, interethnic, and interracial strife. Thus the questions raised by *The Fox from Up Above and the Fox from Down Below* haunt not only discourse about the nation or analyses of hybridity, mestizaje, or transculturation, but life at the beginning of the twenty-first century.

notes

1. The Semantic Space of the Nation

1. Following Reginald Horsman (1981, 305 n. 1), I am using the term "racialist" rather than "racist" when referring to the pseudoscientific racially based theories developed during the nineteenth century.

2. In this chapter, I deal mainly with hybridity and transculturation, since these are terms that either originated in Latin America or have become central to the self-reflection on the area's heterogeneity. Three other terms frequently used to analyze heterogeneity are acculturation, syncretism, and creolization. A useful study of the terminology used in anthropology to study cultural mixture, though marred by a superficial knowledge of Latin American and especially Spanish American history, is Stewart's "Syncretism and Its Synonyms" (1999).

3. *Merriam-Webster's Collegiate Dictionary,* 10th ed., defines "acculturation" as "cultural modification of an individual, group, or people by adapting to or borrowing traits from another culture; *also:* a merging of cultures as a result of prolonged contact"; and as "the process by which a human being acquires the culture of a particular society from infancy."

As Malinowski ([1940] 1995, lviii) points out, however, "The word acculturation implies, because of the preposition *ad* with which it starts, the idea of a *terminus ad quem.* The 'uncultured' is to receive the benefits of 'our culture'; it is he who must change and become converted into one of us."

4. All translations from Rama's *Transculturación narrativa* are mine. (Whenever possible I have used existing translations of the texts quoted. In cases where an English-language source is not indicated, the translation is mine.)

5. Regarding this rediscovery of elements within traditional cultures, Rama (1982, 30) writes, "After self-reflective examination and the selection of its still-valid elements, one attends to the rediscovery of aspects that, while belonging to the traditional inheritance, had not been used previously in a systematic manner and whose expressive possibilities become evident from the modernizing perspective."

6. In evaluating the Latin American literary theory of the 1970s and 1980s (of which Rama's is one of the most important examples), Antonio Cornejo Polar (1999, 9) complained that "it made use of the most flamboyant but less accurate thesis of dependency theory—and we now know this was a dead end."

7. The lack of agency of the periphery is evident in the following classic exposition of dependency theory:

> Dependency is a situation in which the economy of a certain group of countries is conditioned by the development and expansion of another economy to which the former is submitted. The relation of interdependency between two or more economies, and between these and world commerce, assumes the form of dependency when some countries (the dominant ones) are able to expand and self-propel themselves, while the other countries (the dependent ones) can only do so as a result of that expansion, which can act positively or negatively on its immediate development. (dos Santos 1970, 45)

8. Among the questions raised by Rama's analyses is that of the relation between the "transcultural" intellectuals and the traditional cultures that they attempt to modernize. In other words, Rama's analyses do not fully explain how transcultural cultural products, such as novels, impact the ability of a traditional population to modify the social and economic process of modernization.

9. García Canclini does not present modern and postmodern as opposed. On the contrary, he sees the postmodern as "a way of problematizing the equivocal links that the latter has formed with the traditions it tried to exclude or overcome in constituting itself" (García Canclini 1995, 9). Therefore, postmodernity is itself an interpretation of modernity.

10. García Canclini (1995, 277) writes, "The artisans of Ocumicho and Ameyalpetec, the writers of the northern borders of Mexico, Zabala, and Borges, Fontanarrosa and a great many authors of graffiti are liminal artists."

11. García Canclini's use of the words "hybrid" and "hybridity" to analyze postmodern heterogeneity and cultural mixture has been criticized because these words originated in the discourse of scientific racialism (an oxymoron if there ever were one). But the use of these terms has a precedent in the writings on transculturation. For instance, Rama uses "hybrid" in the passage quoted in this chapter. Despite the occasional negative comments that García's use of the word "hybridity" has occasioned, it is justified not only by the fact that his critics appear to propose a semantic determinism that curiously resembles racialism's absurd biological determinism, but also by its history in Latin American discussions of culture. For a critique of the use of "hybrid" and "hybridity," see Michaelsen 1998, par. 5–11.

12. García Canclini (1995, 240) speaks of the process of reterritorialization as being concerned with "questions about identity and the national, the defense of sovereignty, and the unequal appropriation of knowledge and art."

13. A more in-depth examination of the links between discussions of Latin American heterogeneity, in particular what I call the discourse of mestizaje, and the Chicano concept of the borderlands is presented in chapters 8 and 9.

14. José David Saldívar's *Border Matters: Remapping American Cultural Studies* (1997) can serve as an example of this privileging of the U.S. side of the U.S.–Mexico border. All of the "hybrid" artistic products analyzed are created by Chicanos.

2. *Latin America and the Discourse of Mestizaje*

1. According to both Raymond Williams and John Ayto, "race" derives from the French word *race,* which in turn derives from the Italian *razza,* both words having approximately the same meaning of "line of descent." The origins of these earlier cognates are unknown, however (Ayto 1990, 428; Williams 1983, 248).

2. On the rise of modern definitions and theories of the nation, see Anderson 1991, 4; and Williams 1983, 213.

3. The Moriscos were the descendants of the Moorish settlers of Spain. On the discriminatory laws against the Moriscos and their ultimate expulsion from Spain, see Lea 1901. On Spanish anti-Semitism, see Nicholls 1993, 267.

4. On the prevalent egalitarianism of the Enlightenment, see Kahn 1995, 26–27; and Young 1995, 32–33.

5. Louis Agassiz, one of the most noted scientists of the nineteenth century, wrote, "With reference to their offspring, the races of men stand . . . to one another in the same relation as different species among animals" (Agassiz and Agassiz 1886, 297). For a history of the rise of scientific racialism, see Horsman 1981, 116–57; and Young 1995, 6–19.

6. Theodor Waitz, one of the few nineteenth-century critics of scientific racialism made explicit the logical consequences of this new scientific doctrine: "If there be various species of mankind, there must be a natural aristocracy among them, a dominant white species as opposed to the lower races who by their origin are destined to serve the nobility of mankind, and may be tamed, trained, and used like domestic animals, or may, according to circumstances be fattened or used for physiological or other experiments without any compunctions" (quoted in Young 1995, 7).

7. The importance of the nation in Herder's thinking is exemplified in the following quotation: "Since the whole human race is not one single homogeneous group, it does not speak one and the same language. The formation of diverse national languages, therefore, is a natural corollary of human diversity" (Herder

1969, 165). One must note, however, that Herder denied any difference in ability or intelligence among different human groups. Nevertheless, his emphasis on national difference, linked to locality and language, as implying profound psychological and behavioral differences among human groups could be used by racialist thinkers. On Herder, see Anderson 1991, 67–68; Horsman 1981, 27; Kahn 1995, 28–30; and Kristeva 1991, 177–80. Young (1995, 36–43) provides a slightly different reading of Herder centered on the tensions between the localist and cosmopolitan strains in his thought.

8. My brief discussion of the "discovery" of the Aryan people and of the role played by linguistics in the development of racial hierarchies is indebted to Horsman's discussion of these topics (Horsman 1981, 33–39).

9. In his old age, Sarmiento explicitly embraced racialism. His final work was *Conflicto y armonías de las razas en América* (1883) an attempt to apply scientific racialism to the analysis of Latin American society.

10. On immigration to Brazil, see Burns 1993, 314–16 and Skidmore 1974, 136–44.

11. It is particularly difficult to assign intellectual priority regarding this redefinition of mestizaje to any particular thinker in Latin America. Two individuals must, however, be singled out for their early advocacy of mestizaje as the basis on which to build Latin American identity. In the case of Brazil, the German Karl Friedrich Phillipp von Martius as early as 1845 was proclaiming Brazil to be multiracial and multiethnic. (Martius will be studied briefly in chapter 4.) In the case of Spanish America, one can argue that the first proponent of mestizaje was Eugenio María de Hostos. In 1871 Hostos, a Puerto Rican critic and political activist then living in Lima, Peru, published an article entitled "El cholo," which begins with a statement summarizing the ideas that would become hegemonic in the twentieth century: "The New World is the furnace where all the races will fuse into each other, where they are already fusing. This work will take a long time, but one can be sure of the goal. To fuse races is to fuse souls, characters, vocations, aptitudes. It leads, therefore, to completion. And to complete is to improve" (Hostos 1939, 152). However, this aspect of Hostos's thought did not have much resonance in the racialist environment of nineteenth-century Latin America.

12. It is important to note that in the newly conquered Spanish colonies not all offspring of Indians and Spaniards were considered mestizos. The term was used in its legal sense only to describe the children of Spaniards and Indians born out of wedlock (see Lira and Muro 1987, 390).

13. The essays of the 1920s written by Mexican intellectual and politician José Vasconcelos illustrate the persistence of racialist values and ideas in much writing about mestizaje. Regarding his contradictory notion of the cosmic race and the persistence of racial hierarchies in his thought, see chapter 8.

14. The following 1904 quotation from González Prada (1976, 333) is illustrative: "If one accepts the division of humanity into superior and inferior and recognizes the superiority of the whites and their consequent right to rule the planet, nothing is more natural than the suppression of the Negro in Africa, the redskin in the United States, the Tagalog in the Philippines, or the Indian in Peru." Manoel Bomfim made a similar analysis of racism in Brazil (see Bomfim 1903, 278).

15. Mariátegui's ambiguous relationship to racialism will be studied in chapter 6. Critics have found similar slippage between race and culture in Mexican postrevolutionary indigenista mestizaje (see Knight 1990, 86–95).

16. After the 1920s, mestizaje became the semiofficial ideology in much of Latin America. The hegemony of mestizaje as an ideology is evidenced by the fact that it is a central aspect of several of the key works of the time, such as Vasconcelos's *The Cosmic Race* (1925), Mariátegui's *Seven Interpretive Essays* (1928), and Víctor Raúl Haya de la Torre's, *Por la emancipación de América Latina* (1926). In the case of Brazil, it was Gilberto Freyre's work *The Masters and the Slaves* (1933) that brought to the cultural forefront the contribution of Amerindians and especially blacks to Brazilian nationality.

3. *Ricardo Palma's* Tradiciones peruanas

1. The viceroyalty of Peru included all of Spanish South America from the second half of the sixteenth century until the viceroyalties of New Granada and La Plata, constituted by the mainland Caribbean and Río de la Plata areas, were formed in 1739 and 1776 respectively.

2. On the chaotic first decades of Peruvian history, see Losada 1983, 42, 47–51; and Ricardo Palma's "La bohemia de mi tiempo" (1953, p. 1293).

3. The first edition of *Tradiciones peruanas* was published in 1872. However, the first of the heterogeneous texts that Palma collected in *Tradiciones peruanas* appeared in magazines in 1854. Therefore, Palma's *Tradiciones peruanas* have their beginning within the period between 1848 and 1860, which he designated as that of the *bohemios*. (*Tradiciones peruanas completas,* a compilation of all of Palma's tradiciones and of his most significant essays and articles was first published in 1953.)

4. Most attempts at defining the tradición as a genre have not been much more than extended descriptions. For examples see Compton 1982, 25–35; and Oviedo 1965, 146–68.

5. The corregidor presided over the government of a town and was responsible for all judicial matters. The position of corregidor had as one of its principal obligations the protection of the local Indians. Since the corregidor was responsible only to the Spanish crown and, therefore, was free from local control, abuses of power were common. In the case of Arriaga, the tradición notes that he

"abused Europeans and criollos whom he considered to be plebeians," and also was "cruel towards the Indians" (Palma 1953, 685).

6. The tradición describes those present during the celebration as "the most notable neighbors of the parish" (Palma 1953, 684). Therefore, it is logical to assume that the group would include criollos and even Spaniards.

7. For another example of Palma's egalitarian treatment of Indian characters, see his portrayal of Catalina Huanca in "Los tesoros de Catalina Huanca" (1877). For a significant example of Palma's egalitarian treatment of black characters, see "Un negro en el sillón presidencial" (1910). (Both are in the 1953 edition of *Tradiciones peruanas*.)

8. For a list of the crónicas that present versions of this story, see Arrom 1991, 155 n. 60.

9. An encomienda was a grant of Indian labor made by the Spanish crown. The stated purpose of the encomienda was the catechization of the Indians—for whose evangelization the encomendero was responsible. In practice, the encomienda was a hidden form of slavery.

10. Cornejo writes, "In fact, when Palma almost surreptitiously displaces Quechua and transforms it into Spanish, he is producing a homogeneous space, without fissures, precisely where the most dangerous fissures divide the national community" (Cornejo Polar 1994, 111).

11. The other important study of this tradición, Raquel Chang-Rodríguez's "Elaboración de fuentes en 'Carta canta' y 'Papelito jabla lengua,'" is principally a comparison of Palma's and Álvaro de la Iglesias's tradiciones with the version of the story found in the Inca Garcilaso's *Comentarios reales* (which Chang-Rodríguez considers to be the source of both nineteenth-century texts).

12. In his "Neologismos y americanismos" (1895), Palma (1953, 1379) writes, "The academies are like congresses, and must write their constitutions and laws (I mean their dictionaries and grammars) taking into account the customs of the people, the natural spirit of progress, and above all, common usage."

13. Referring to Solar, the narrator states that "although he was not among Pizarro's companions in Cajamarca, he arrived in time to receive a good portion in the division of goods of the conquest" (Palma 1953, 147).

14. According to the narrator of "Carta Canta," the Indians claimed that the Spaniards "used those large animals because of their laziness, so as not to have to work" (Palma 1953, 147).

15. Palma in "Refutación a un texto de historia" (1886) characterizes the encomienda and the resistance of the conquistadors against Blasco Núñez de Vela's attempts to enforce the Leyes de Indias with the following words: "So unbearable must have been the encomiendas and the *mitas* [forced labor], and the encomenderos so extreme in their abuses and cruelty, that the king, alarmed by the continuous complaints sent from here by men of goodwill, sent Viceroy

Blasco Nuñez to enforce regulations that the encomenderos refused to obey, instead rebelling under Gonzalo and Girón" (Palma 1953, 1481–82).

16. As Chang-Rodríguez (1971, 434) writes, "How can the latecomer Antonio Solar, whose property had such dubious origin and whose conduct had defied authority, chastise his Indians calling them 'thieves' and 'rogues'? Palma, by giving information and with a simple characterization, places Don Antonio and the aborigines at the same level." (My analysis of the description in "Carta canta" of the conquistadors as exploitative has drawn on Chang-Rodríguez's brief but lucid comments in "Elaboración de fuentes" [1971]).

4. *José de Alencar's* Iracema

1. The following passage from Martius's 1845 essay illustrates his approach to Brazilian history and identity: "Anyone who undertakes to write the history of Brazil, a country which promises so much, should never lose sight of the elements which contributed to the development of man there. These diverse elements come from the three races, namely: the copper-colored, or American; the white or Caucasian; and the black, or Ethiopian. Because of the reciprocal and changing relations of the three races, the present population consists of a novel mixture, whose history therefore has a particular stamp" (Martius 1967, 23).

2. The exclusion of blacks from Alencar's novels has been attributed to his own politically conservative and pro-slavery position (Sommer 1991, 156–61).

3. Alencar's works have had great popular success. In fact, *Iracema,* with more than one hundred editions, is possibly the most popular book in Brazilian history (Schwamborn 1990, 172). Many critics, while admitting the historical importance of his work, compare Alencar's novels unfavorably with the sophisticated narratives of his friend and admirer Machado de Assis. *Iracema* is, however, the exception to this rule. Even critics, such as Alfredo Bosi or Ria Lemaire, who complain of Alencar's lack of psychological perception or his conservative political positions, describe *Iracema* as a masterpiece (see Bosi 1970, 148–55; Lemaire 1989, 69; Sommer 1991, 140–42; Valente 1994, 142–43).

4. Clifford Landers's translation (Alencar 2000) omits this subtitle.

5. As Alencar himself admits in his "Historical Argument"—a lengthy footnote in the novel—it was Pero Coelho who actually founded Ceará in 1603. But since this first settlement was abandoned, Alencar proposes Martim Moreno's second foundation of Ceará in 1611 as the fictional origin of this state and, implicitly, of Brazil.

6. This aspect of *Iracema*'s plot follows popular Romantic-era story lines exemplified by the novels of Châteaubriand and Bernardin de Saint-Pierre and, in opera, by Bellini's *Norma* (see Campos 1993, 16; Sommer 1991, 363 n. 38; Wasserman 1994, 188).

7. Ria Lemaire (1989, 63) describes Moacir's fate from this perspective: "The

child—her child—has been educated by non-Indians; he has lost the memory of his mother and of his origins." See also Haberly (1983, 50).

8. This fact has been noticed by other critics. For instance, Alcides Villaça (2000, 142) notes that "up to a certain point in the novel . . . Martim is under the brave and watchful protection of Iracema . . . and . . . from the middle to the end of the novel all the initiative passes to Martim."

9. "Iracema's 'savage condition' freed Alencar from his conservative inhibitions and from the prejudices of his epoch, allowing him to create a female figure capable of amorous initiatives and sexual realizations" (Campos 1993, 17 n. 6).

10. Alencar's interest in creating a myth is already clear in his subtitle for the novel: "Lenda do Ceará." Several critics have emphasized *Iracema*'s mythic aspects, including Haberly 1983, 48–49; Lemaire 1989, 60–61; and Zilberman 1977, 148–52.

11. *Iracema* reverses the structure of *O Guarani,* in which the bulk of the narrative takes place in a historical world marked by the opposition between the Portuguese and the Aimoré Indians but concludes with a mythic flood that permits Peri and Cecilia (possibly) to become a Brazilian Adam and Eve.

12. The following quotation from Ricardo Palma's "López de Aguirre, el traidor," (1906) one of his *Tradiciones peruanas,* is exemplary of the intense condemnation of the conquistadors that one can on occasion find among Spanish American writers: "Extremely prolific in crimes and evildoers was the sixteenth century in Peru. It seems as if Spain had opened the doors of its prisons and its inmates had escaped to these regions. The horrors of the conquest, the wars between followers of Pizarro and Almagro, and the evil deeds of Godines during the revolts in Potosi give the impression after three centuries of the creations of a febrile imagination" (Palma 1953, 74).

13. In *Ubirajara,* Alencar criticizes colonial descriptions of Amerindian life by pointing out that "the invading race attempted to justify their cruelty by lowering the aborigines to the condition of beasts that it was necessary to hunt" ([1874] 1977, 168 n. 53).

5. *Gilberto Freyre's* Casa-Grande e Senzala

1. *Casa-Grande e Senzala,* which literally translates as "The Plantation House and the Slave Quarters," appeared in English as *The Masters and the Slaves* (1956). Given the fact that the spatial opposition present in the original title plays a minor role in my argument, I have decided to use the Portuguese title throughout my essay. Unless otherwise noted, all quotations from Freyre's study are taken from the English translation.

2. Amado wrote the following about *Casa-Grande e Senzala:* "No book shook Brazil like Gilberto Freyre's first; no work influenced public opinion so

profoundly nor contributed to the development of Brazilian writing and reading" (quoted in Coutinho 1994, 14). Antônio Candido ([1967] 1995, 10) has written about "the revolutionary force and the liberating impact of this great book." Darcy Ribeiro (1986, 110–11) considered Freyre to be as great an influence on Brazil "in the cultural field as Cervantes in Spain, Camões in Lusitania, Tolstoy in Russia, Sartre in France." Filmmaker Nelson Pereira dos Santos declared that "I usually say that Brazil has two founders: Gilberto Freyre and Jorge Amado" (quoted in Rangel 1997).

3. For a balanced—and brief—description of Alencar's political activities and their relationship to his exclusion of black characters from his "foundational" novels, see Sommer (1991, 156–61). Sommer (1991, 160) also writes about Alencar's "sliding between one racial category and another, substituting Indians for blacks." There is textual basis for this interpretation. In Alencar's *O Guarani,* Peri, the Indian protagonist, is described as "a friendly slave" (Alencar [1857] 1994, 280).

4. Stam (1997, 331) describes this common—and absurd—stereotype of blacks as "narcissistic projections of whites . . . these emblems of happy servility represent the slaves as the masters desired them to be."

5. Palmares had a population of approximately twenty thousand people. On Palmares, see Burns 1993, 46–47.

6. Freyre himself emphasized the influence of Boas in his theoretical differentiation between race and culture (Freyre 1956, xxvii).

7. This virulently racist passage is omitted in Samuel Putnam's (1956) English translation. The place in the text where it would have been included is marked by a footnote that defends Freyre's representation of the Jews by emphasizing his sporadic criticisms of Portuguese and Jesuit anti-Semitism (Freyre 1956, 230 n. 5).

8. Ribeiro (1986, 141–46) has criticized the marginalization of Indian achievements, particularly in agriculture, as well as the reduction of the Indian to stereotypes.

9. Freyre was the organizer of the first Congresso Afro-Brasileiro, which also played a significant role in promoting awareness of the impact of African cultures in Brazil (Freyre [1933] 1995, xi).

10. Skidmore (1974, 192) claims that the effect of *Casa-Grande e Senzala* "was to reinforce the whitening ideal by showing graphically that the (primarily white) elite had gained valuable cultural traits from their intimate contact with the African (and Indian to a lesser extent)."

11. On the issue of class in *Casa-Grande e Senzala,* see Medeiros 1984, 30; and Mota 1980, 57. For a critique of Freyre's vision of Brazil as exemplifying racial harmony, see Nascimento and Nascimento 1992, 109–10.

12. The Portuguese original reads, "O furor femeeiro do português se terá exercido sobre vítimas nem sempre confraternizantes no gozo." Putnam translates this passage differently: "The furious passions of the Portuguese must have been vented upon victims who did not always share his sexual tastes" (Freyre 1956, 75).

13. Freyre (1956, 85) writes about this imagined generalized loss of sexual restraint during the Portuguese colonization, "No sooner had the European leaped ashore than he found his feet slipping among the naked Indian women. . . . The women were the first to offer themselves to the whites."

14. For brief analyses of syphilis in *Casa-Grande e Senzala,* see Araújo 1994, 62; and Arroyo 1993, 39–40.

15. On malnutrition, see Freyre 1956, 60.

16. The English version of Freyre's text, *The Masters and the Slaves,* has as its subtitle *A Study in the Development of Brazilian Civilization.*

17. It is important to note that Freyre (1956, 85) is aware of "a fact that appears to me linked naturally to the economic circumstances that shaped our patriarchal society; the fact that the woman in Brazil is so often the helpless victim of the male's domination or abuse." This awareness does not inhibit the frequently celebratory tone used in his descriptions of the patriarchal family.

18. The use of psychological explanations for social situations has been pointed out by Medeiros (1984, 58–60).

19. Freyre's descriptions of Indian and black male sexuality are fully concordant with the feminization of Indians and blacks. He emphasizes the supposed weakness of sexual desire among Indian men and even believes that they possess smaller-than-average sexual organs (Freyre 1956, 97–98). Freyre gives a very similar description of black male sexuality: "enormous giants who had the penis of a small boy" (p. 428).

20. It is important to note that Freyre's first person plural assumes that the reader is white and male. This significant aspect of Freyre's narrative strategy will be analyzed later. (This identification of the reader with the white male was noted in passing by Doris Sommer 1991, 364 n. 59.)

21. Freyre's own political career managed to reconcile antiracism with a defense of colonialism. From being antiracist and antifascist and having links to the Esquerda Democrática in his youth, he became a defender of Portuguese colonialism in Africa and of the military dictatorship in Brazil in the 1960s and 1970s (see Coutinho 1994, 7–8; Mota 1980, 70–73).

6. *José Carlos Mariátegui*

1. On the posthumous evaluation of Mariátegui's writings and political work by the Communist International, see Flores Galindo 1980, 106–8.

2. According to the Worldcat online database (accessed August 29, 2000),

forty-two books on Maríategui have been published since 1994, the year of the centennial of his birth.

3. Mariátegui's *Seven Interpretive Essays on Peruvian Reality* (1928), his most celebrated work, begins with an epigraph from Nietzsche. His interest in psychoanalysis led Mariátegui to publish an early translation of Freud in his magazine *Amauta* and to refer to psychoanalytical concepts throughout his works. For a study of the relationship between Nietzsche and Mariátegui, see Ofelia Schutte's *Cultural Identity and Social Liberation in Latin American Thought* (1993, 27–29, 41–49). On Mariátegui's interest in Freud see Flores Galindo's "Uchuraccay: el psicoanálisis como metáfora" (1988, 180–82) and *La agonía de Mariátegui* (1980, 101). (Sorel's influence on Mariátegui will be briefly discussed later.)

4. The ending of Mariátegui's *Seven Interpretive Essays* is an example of his interest in eliminating the binary oppositions that had characterized Latin American culture: "The universal, ecumenical roads we have chosen to travel, and for which we are reproached, take us ever closer to ourselves" (Mariátegui 1971, 287).

5. *Seven Interpretive Essays on Peruvian Reality* (1971), the English translation of Mariátegui's *Siete ensayos de interpretación de la realidad peruana,* follows the original 1928 Spanish-language edition and does not include this passage, which was originally part of an article titled "Sobre el problema indígena. Sumaria revisión histórica," published in 1928. The Amauta editions of Mariátegui's *Siete ensayos* have included the original Spanish version of this essay—now titled "Sumaria revisión histórica"—since the first posthumous printing in 1943 (see Mariátegui [1928] 1981, 44 n).

6. It is important to note that in "Literature on Trial," Mariátegui made several significant exceptions to this apparently complete rejection of previous Peruvian intellectuals. The authors rescued from Mariátegui's condemnation are Mariano Melgar, Ricardo Palma, Manuel Gonzáles Prada, and Federico More.

7. The influence of his European stay on his adoption of Marxism is made clear in this well-known autobiographical statement included on the inside cover of the Amauta edition of the *Siete ensayos:* "I lived for two years in Italy, where I acquired a wife and some ideas" (Mariátegui [1928] 1981, my translation).

8. In his *La agonía de Mariátegui,* Flores Galindo (1980, 28) comments on the abstract analysis of Latin America made by the Communist International: "For the Komintern there were only 'semi-colonial' countries, defined by a specific relationship of dependency to imperialist capital, and it was this condition . . . that permitted the development of tactics and strategies defined at a continental level. There were no specifically national traits. Peru was the same as Mexico or Argentina."

9. In "The Indigenous Question"—an incomplete translation of Mariátegui's and Pesce's "El problema de las razas en América Latina" (1929)—Mariátegui expresses his optimism regarding the revolutionary potential of the Indian

population of Peru: "Perhaps an indigenous revolutionary consciousness will form slowly, but once the Indians have made the socialist ideal their own, they will serve it with a discipline, tenacity, and strength that few proletarians from other milieus will be able to surpass" (Mariátegui and Pesce 1996, 108).

10. On the Third International's analysis of Latin American feudalism, see Flores Galindo (1980, 30–31).

11. The Spanish original from *Siete ensayos* is, "Esta corriente encuentra un estímulo en la asimilación por nuestra cultura de elementos de cosmopolitismo" ([1928] 1981, 329). The English edition of *Seven Interpretive Essays* renders this as follows: "This current, moreover, is encouraged by the elements of cosmopolitanism that have been assimilated into our literature" (Mariátegui 1971, 269).

12. See Mariátegui's essay "The Programmatic Principles of the Socialist Party" (1928), regarding the party he founded (in Mariátegui 1996, 92–93).

13. Octavio Paz has complained about a popular version of Mexican history according to which "Mexico was born with the Aztec state, or even earlier; it lost its independence in the sixteenth century and recovered it in 1821. According to this idea, between Aztec and modern Mexico there is not only continuity but identity; both are the same nation, which is why we say that Mexico recovered her independence in 1821. New Spain was an interregnum, a historical parenthesis, a vacuum in which nothing of importance occurred. It was the period of the Mexican nation's bondage" (Paz 1988, 11). The similarities between this popular version of the discourse of mestizaje and Mariátegui's analysis of Peruvian history and future are evident.

14. The Spanish original reads, "Sobre la tierra virginal de América, de donde borraron toda huella indígena, los colonizadores anglosajones echaron desde su arribo los cimientos del orden capitalista" (Mariátegui 1981a, 148). Michael Pearlman's translation in *The Heroic and Creative Meaning of Socialism,* while not inaccurate, loses some of the connotations I refer to in my analysis: "Upon their arrival in the virginal land of America, from which they expunged all indigenous vestiges, the Anglo-Saxon colonizers laid the foundations of the capitalist order" (1996, 26).

15. According to the *Pequeño Larrouse ilustrado* (1990) among the meanings of *virgen* are "selva virgen, la todavía sin explorar" and "tierra virgen la que nunca ha sido cultivada" ("virgin jungle that has not been explored" and "virgin land that has never been cultivated").

16. The English edition translates *potente* as powerful (Mariátegui 1971, 125). I have modified the translation in order to maintain the sexual connotation. The Spanish original reads, "El colonizador anglosajón no encontró en el territorio norteamericano ni una cultura avanzada ni una población potente" ([1928] 1981, 163).

17. I have provided my own translation for this passage because the English

edition of Mariátegui's text fuses this sentence with a previous one. "Zambo" refers to the offspring of black and Indian parents. The Spanish original reads, "El negro, el mulato, el 'zambo' representan en nuestro pasado, elementos coloniales."

18. The Chinese are described as bringing to Peru "the fatalism, apathy, and defects of the decrepit Orient" (Mariátegui 1971, 279).

19. Even in the case of these two books, Mariátegui claimed in the author's note to the *Seven Interpretive Essays* that they were not "organic" books, but rather were written "spontaneously and without premeditation" (1971, xxxv). Mariátegui prepared but did not publish during his lifetime *Defensa del marxismo* and wrote an "organic" book, *Ideología y política,* that unfortunately was lost for unknown reasons. (A collection of essays and political writings has been published with the title *Ideología y política* [1980], but this should not be confused with the lost work.) On Mariátegui's lost book, see Flores Galindo (1980, 101–4).

20. The rendering of this passage in *Seven Interpretive Essays* differs substantively from the Spanish original. The Spanish text reads, "Sólo el socialismo, despertando en él conciencia clasista, es capaz de conducirlo a la ruptura definitive con los últimos rezagos de espíritu colonial." The English edition mistranslates this passage as, "The Negro and mulatto can be redeemed only through a social and economic revolution that will turn them into workers and thereby gradually extirpate their slave mentality" (1971, 273).

21. For instance, in the Spanish original of *Seven Interpretive Essays,* Mariátegui's negative evaluation of the influence of blacks in Peru concludes with a condemnation of racialism as "razonamientos zootécnicos" ([1928] 1981, 341–43). The English version of Mariátegui's text translates this phrase, strangely enough, as "zoological conditions" (1971, 281). A more exact translation would be "zootechnical reasoning."

22. On contemporary cultural racism, see Kahn 1995, 6–7, 125–26.

7. The Black Song of Los Van Van

1. Juan Formell, Los Van Van's founder and leader, has acknowledged on numerous occasions the influence of U.S. music on the band. For instance, during an interview on Uruguayan radio, he stated that "Los Van Van began during a period in which people did not want to dance to Cuban music; then, what I did was to mix the pop music of the time with our roots, such as the Cuban *son,* and immediately people fell in love with our work" (Formell 1998).

2. This sentence is spoken by lead singer Mario Rivera just before he begins to sing. The booklet accompanying the compact disc includes only a partial transcription of the lyrics in Spanish; therefore, all translations are mine.

3. The meaning of *la cubana* is ambiguous. While Rivera's phrasing links la cubana with the previously mentioned "mulatto woman," he could just as easily

be referring to the subsequent "different mixture" (in other words, to either Cuban culture or race).

4. *Clave* are percussion sticks that mark the beat (3/2) of the entire song. (The mention of the "magic of the three plus two" in the lyrics is a reference to this clave beat.)

5. The lyrics analyzed in this chapter are a transcription of those sung by Rivera, which are not included in printed lyrics in the booklet. I do not know whether these additional lyrics were written by Formell, improvised by the vocalist during live performances and incorporated in the song, or simply improvised by the vocalist during the recording. I will provide and translate these lyrics as needed.

6. On la mulata and el negrito and their role as representations of racial stereotypes, consult Robin Moore's *Nationalizing Blackness* (1997) and Vera M. Kutzinki's *Sugar's Secrets* (1993). Kutzinki's text is an in-depth analysis of the figure of the mulata, particularly as a negative racial stereotype. She does not deal with the negrito and deals only briefly with the teatro vernáculo.

7. On the centrality of African religions to Afro-Cuban culture, see Benítez Rojo (1996, 52).

8. Nueva trova is the Cuban art song movement associated with the revolution. Its two best-known singers and composers are Silvio Rodríguez and Pablo Milanés.

9. On Vasconcelos's Hispanism, see chapter 8.

8. *Richard Rodriguez in "Borderland"*

1. Throughout this chapter, I follow Richard Rodriguez's own unaccented spelling of his last name.

2. Among the critics identified with the Chicano and Mexican American community who have given a positive reception to Rodriguez's writings, Ilan Stavans, José David Saldívar, and Rubén Martínez stand out. Stavans, while critical of *Days of Obligation*'s historical analysis, is very sympathetic to Rodriguez as a Mexican American writer. He claims that Rodriguez is "the embodiment of that complex fate shared by those born twice American: hybrids always living in the hyphen, with one leg here and the other across the Rio Grande" (Stavans 1993, 26). Moreover, Stavans emphatically states, "Rodriguez is not any sort of right-winger" (p. 21). Saldívar (1997, 150) includes *Days of Obligation* with Rubén Martínez's *The Other Side* and the performance works of Guillermo Gómez Peña as examples of this new non-essentialist and non-racialist border literature. In his review of *Days of Obligation,* Martínez claims to have discovered that he and Rodriguez "have always lived on the same side of the border" (quoted in Saldívar 1997, 210–11 n. 10).

3. Regarding Rodriguez's political points of view, in an interview with

Christopher Caldwell, published in the *Washington Times' Insight on the News* on 4 January 1993, Rodriguez claimed to be "more patient with conservatives" than with liberals, and said that "Bush had in many ways an admirable record" (Rodriguez 1993, 14). In the same interview, however, he declared that, given the Republican attacks on gay rights, he would not vote for Bush. (The relevance of Rodriguez's gay identity to the changes in his thought is analyzed later in this essay.) Despite his basic sympathy for the Republican Party, Rodriguez has collaborated with progressive magazines such as *Mother Jones* and is currently a contributing editor to the Pacific News Service, a liberal organization for which Rubén Martínez writes.

William Nericcio (1994, 141), for instance, finds Rodriguez to be "like some mutation born of Roy Cohn and Jack Webb" policing "the precincts of the Americas." Scott Michaelsen (1998, par. 17), in his analysis of Saldívar's reevaluation of Rodriguez in *Border Matters,* comes to the conclusion that Rodriguez "remains a bitter foe of liberalism in all guises." Some of Rodriguez's essays defending illegal immigration are "Prophets without Papers" (1995b) and "The New Native Americans" (1995d). On gay rights, see his television essay "Language or Silence" (1998d).

4. Gustavo Pérez Firmat (1996, 263) has noted that "part of the problem with *Hunger of Memory* . . . may be that Rodríguez attributes to culture conflicts and insecurities that have rather—or also—to do with gender."

5. Rodriguez's comparison with Paz is misleading in the sense that *Hunger of Memory,* unlike *The Labyrinth of Solitude,* presents itself primarily as an autobiography rather than as an objective study of national identity. There is however an evident intertextual relationship between the two texts that has been analyzed by other authors; see Perera 1993, 63; and Pérez Firmat 1996, 262.

6. Vasconcelos identified the American continent with the mythical Atlantis.

7. Vasconcelos compares the colonizations of the United States and Latin America as the moments that determined the two areas' national and regional traits: "Spanish colonization created mixed races, this signals its character, fixes its responsibility, and defines its future. The English kept on mixing only with the whites and annihilated the natives. Even today, they continue to annihilate them in a sordid and economic fight, more efficient yet than armed conquest" (Vasconcelos 1997, 18).

8. The following quotation is an example of the extremes that Vasconcelos's racism could reach. Regarding the process of miscegenation that would lead to the formation of the cosmic race, he writes: "The lower types of the species will be absorbed by the superior type. In this manner, for example, the Black could be redeemed, and step by step, by voluntary extinction, the uglier stocks will give way to the more handsome" (Vasconcelos 1997, 32).

9. One must also oppose Rodriguez's view to that of Octavio Paz, who describes Malinche, identified with the mythical *chingada,* as "pure passivity": "The *chingón* [fucker] is the *macho,* the male, he rips open the *chingada* [the fucked one], the female, who is pure passivity, defenseless against the exterior world" (Paz 1985, 77). Later in the essay, Paz identifies the chingada with Malinche: "If the Chingada is a representation of the violated Mother, it is appropriate to associate her with the Conqu
est, which was also a violation, not only in a historical sense but also in the very flesh of Indian women. The symbol of this violation is doña Malinche, the mistress of Cortés (p. 86).

Rodriguez is aware of the way his own interpretation of the cosmic race and mestizaje differs from Vasconcelos's and Paz's. In *Days of Obligation,* he writes, "Mexican philosophers powwow in their tony journals about Indian 'fatalism' and 'Whither Mexico?' *El fatalismo del indio* is an important Mexican philosophical theme; the phrase is trusted to conjure the quality of Indian passivity as well as to initiate debate about Mexico's reluctant progress toward modernization" (Rodriguez 1992, 2).

10. During a 1995 interview in *America,* Rodriguez reaffirmed his identification with the Indian. When asked by Paul Crowley, "Do you think of yourself as an Indian?," Rodriguez responded: "Yes, I do—though only lately. . . I began rethinking the Indian role in history as the 500th anniversary of the Columbus landing approached. I kept hearing all this white guilt about what the European did to the poor Indian. I was in Mexico City one day when I had my 'vision': In the capital of Spanish colonialism there were Indian faces like mine everywhere. Where, then, was the conquistador?" (Rodriguez 1995c, 8).

11. Vasconcelos (1997, 17) writes of "that abundance of love that allowed the Spaniard to create a new race with the Indian and the Black, profusely spreading white ancestry through the soldier who begat a native family."

12. Rodriguez has made this association between Mexico and the feminine clearer in his essay on *subcomandante* Marcos: "Mexicans have struggled, for centuries, to accept the implications of their nation's femininity" (1995a, 1).

13. Pérez Firmat has noted the incongruity of Rodriguez's identification with Caliban in *Hunger of Memory:* "Not only is the admission of book theft suspect, but the invocation of Caliban in the very first sentence as if he were the author's brutish muse does not square with the book's tone and content" (Pérez Firmat 1996, 257).

14. He writes about his homosexuality in two of the chapters of *Days of Obligation:* "Late Victorians" and "The Latin American Novel." His coming out has been criticized for being unwilling to "embrace life" (Michaelsen 1998, par. 15). The ambiguity of his public statements, together with the increase in antigay rhetoric and action, may have prompted his second, more emphatic coming out

in his television essay "Language or Silence," broadcast on "The NewsHour with Jim Lehrer," on 15 September 1998. There, he unequivocally states: "I say it today. I am gay. I toss the word in the air. I say it in the plain light of day. Brutally, I force this word upon you. I say it in a louder voice: I am gay. It is in your power to accept my sentence as meaningful or appropriate in this public moment, or to resist it, to turn away toward silence, to make me invisible" (Rodriguez 1998d).

15. Other historians include the north of Mexico in the borderlands, see, e.g., Gibson 1966, 182. For a thorough discussion of the history of these concepts, see Driscoll 1993, 1–20. (The history of the concepts of the borderlands and the border presented in this essay is based on Driscoll's study.)

16. This was a literature about Mexicans and Mexican Americans written by mainstream Anglo writers for mainstream Anglo readers. This literature of the borderlands was more concerned with the escapist needs of North American readers than with the faithful representation of Mexican or Mexican American points of view (see Driscoll 1993, 11, 13–15).

17. Among many sources for maps of the borderlands is Gibson 1966, 184.

18. Saldívar, for one, is aware of the differences between his use of the borderlands and those of earlier historians like Bolton: "Needless to say, my view of the U.S.–Mexican borderlands differs from the sentimentalized 'fantasy history' of the Spanish borderlands constructed (between 1911 and 1965) by Bolton and his students and the University of California at Berkeley" (Saldívar 1997, 201 n. 2). My analysis of theories of the borderlands is far from exhaustive. It does, however, attempt to point out some of the central traits associated with this Chicano analytical paradigm.

19. Rafael Pérez-Torres (1997, 34) has written about Anzaldúa, "No Chicana author is associated with the borderlands more than Gloria Anzaldúa. Caught between the worlds of lesbian and straight, Mexican and American, First World and Third World, Anzaldúa's writing seems to exemplify and reflect the condition of the interstitial and liminal—of being between and on the threshold." Not all Chicano critics have been receptive to the "borderlands" paradigms. For a negative reflection on Anzaldúa's foundational role in the contemporary notion of the borderlands, see Limón 1998, 157.

20. Saldívar's conceptualization of the borderland—and the analyses he bases on it—have an additional source: García Canclini's *Hybrid Cultures* (1995). However, Saldívar relocates hybridity from Latin America and the Mexican side of the U.S.–Mexico border to the Chicano communities. On García Canclini, see chapter 1.

21. While Anzaldúa refers approvingly to Vasconcelos's concept of the cosmic race, the consequence of miscegenation in *Borderlands/La Frontera* is psychological heterogeneity rather than biological homogeneity: "From this racial, ideological, cultural, and biological crosspollinization, an 'alien' consciousness, is

presently in the making—a new mestiza consciousness, *una conciencia de mujer.* It is a consciousness of the Borderlands" (Anzaldúa 1987, 77). This aspect of Anzaldúa's thought is explored in somewhat greater detail in chapter 9.

22. One can, however, argue that the notion of the borderlands, if pushed to its extreme, leads to conclusions reminiscent of Rodriguez's homogeneous hybridity in that they ultimately undermine the explicit celebration of cultural diversity and the policies and politics of multiculturalism. Economic and cultural globalization, and the mainstream economic policies associated with them, lead to the proliferation of border experiences no longer exclusively associated with specific geographical regions (such as the U.S.–Mexico border) or populations (for instance Chicanos). This aspect of the borderlands will be explored at greater length in chapter 9.

23. Rodriguez's response to the recent (1997) debate on bilingual education can serve as an example of the less-strident tone that now characterizes his response to progressive public policies. Rodriguez, throughout his career a staunch critic of bilingual education, concludes his television essay "Speaking American" by presenting the debate for or against this policy as antiquated: "Bilingual education—¿Sí or no? For me, it is more important to take my place proudly in line with Lithuanian grandmothers and Vietnamese grandfathers, to say with Walt Whitman, 'I speak American'" (Rodriguez 1998c).

9. *From Mestizaje to Multiculturalism*

1. Keep in mind that Arguedas's masterwork, *Deep Rivers* (1958), is the privileged example used by Ángel Rama in *Transculturación narrativa en América Latina.*

2. I have modified the English translation in order to bring it closer to the Spanish original. The original reads, "Aquí en Chimbote, la mayor gente barriada nos hemos, más o menos, igualado estos últimos años estos; nos hemos igualado en la miseria miserableza que sera más pesadazo en sus apariencias, padre, que en las alturas sierra, porque aquí está reunido la gente desabandonada del Dios y mismo de la tierra, porque ya nadies es de ninguna parte-pueblo en barriadas de Chimbote." The English version, for some strange reason, assigns responsibility for bringing people to the shanty towns to one of the characters, Father Cardozo (Arguedas 2000, 243).

3. The title of Arguedas's posthumous novel refers to the pre-Columbian myth of the two foxes that represented the division of Peru into a coastal and an Andean region. In this manner, Arguedas's reflections on the cultural and racial heterogeneity of the Peru of his time attempted to connect with what could be seen as the first representation of this plurality.

4. Despite Kristeva's emphasis on the fact that a new "homogeneity is not very likely, perhaps hardly desirable" (Kristeva 1991, 194), it is hard not to

interpret the following statement as implying the loss of significance of cultural difference in contemporary France and Europe: "A paradoxical community is emerging, made up of foreigners who are reconciled with themselves to the extent that they recognize themselves as foreigners. The multinational society would thus be the consequence of extreme individualism, but conscious of its discontents and limits, knowing only indomitable people ready-to-help-themselves in their weakness, a weakness whose other name is our radical strangeness" (p. 195).

works cited

Agassiz, Louis, and Elizabeth Cary Agassiz. 1886. *A Journey in Brazil*. Boston: Houghton.

Alencar, José de. [1857] 1994. *O Guarani*. São Paulo: Editora Ática.

———. [1874] 1977. *Ubirajara*. São Paulo: Editora Ática.

———. 2000. *Iracema: A Novel by José de Alencar*. Translated by Clifford E. Landers. New York: Oxford University Press.

Álvarez, José Rogelio. 1978. *Enciclopedia de México*. Mexico: Enciclopedia de México.

Anderson, Benedict. 1991. *Imagined Communities: Reflections on the Origin and Spread of Nationalism*. 2d. ed. London: Verso.

Anzaldúa, Gloria. 1987. *Borderlands/La Frontera: The New Mestiza*. San Francisco: Aunt Lute.

Araújo, Ricardo Benzaquen de. 1994. *Guerra e paz: 'Casa-Grande e Senzala' e a obra de Gilberto Freyre nos anos 30*. Rio de Janeiro: Editora 34.

Arguedas, José María. [1971] 1992. *El zorro de arriba y el zorro de abajo*. Edited by Eve-Marie Fell. Mexico City: Archivos.

———. 2000. *The Fox from Up Above and the Fox from Down Below*. Translated by Frances Barraclough. Edited by Julio Ortega. Pittsburgh, Pa.: University of Pittsburgh Press.

Arrom, José Juan. 1991. El Inca Garcilaso de la Vega o la crónica como investigación filosófica y comentario social. In *Imaginación del Nuevo Mundo: diez estudios sobre los inicios de la narrativa hispanoamericana,* 137–60. Mexico: Sigloveintiuno.

Arroyo, Jossianna. 1993. El cuerpo del esclavo y la narrativa de la nación en *Casa-Grande e Senzala* de Gilberto Freyre. *Lucero* 4:31–42.

Ayto, John. 1990. *Dictionary of Word Origins*. New York: Arcade Publishing.

Benítez Rojo, Antonio. 1996. *The Repeating Island: The Caribbean and the Postmodern Perspective*. 2d. ed. Translated by James Maraniss. Durham, N.C.: Duke University Press.

Bomfim, Manoel. 1903. *A America Latina, males de origem.* Rio de Janeiro: Garnier.

Bosi, Alfredo. 1970. *Historia concisa da literatura brasileira.* São Paulo: Editôra Cultrix.

Burns, E. Bradford. 1993. *A History of Brazil.* 3d. ed. New York: Columbia University Press.

Bushnell, David, and Neill Macaulay. 1994. *The Emergence of Latin America in the Nineteenth Century.* 2d. ed. New York: Oxford University Press.

Campos, Haroldo de. 1993. *Iracema:* A Vanguard Archaeography. Translated by Randal Johnson. In *Tropical Paths: Essays on Modern Brazilian Literature.* Edited by Randal Johnson, 11–29. New York: Garland.

Candido, Antônio. [1967] 1995. O significado de *Raízes do Brasil.* In *Raízes do Brasil,* by Sérgio Buarque de Holanda, 9–21. São Paulo: Companhia das Letras.

Castillo, Ricardo. 1999. Another Miami Vice. *U.S. News and World Report,* 27 September, p. 37.

Chang-Rodríguez, Raquel. 1971. Elaboración de fuentes en "Carta canta" y "Papelito jabla lengua." *Kentucky Romance Quarterly* 24(4):433–39.

Compton, Merlin D. 1982. *Ricardo Palma.* Boston: Twayne.

Cornejo Polar, Antonio. 1992. Un ensayo sobre los "zorros" de Arguedas. In *El zorro de arriba y el zorro de abajo.* Edited by Eve-Marie Fell, 296–306. Mexico City: Archivos.

——. 1994. *Escribir en el aire: ensayo sobre la heterogeneidad socio-cultural en las literaturas andinas.* Lima: Editorial Horizonte.

——. 1998. Mestizaje e hibridez: los riesgos de las metáforas. *Revista de Crítica Literaria Latinoamericana* 47:7–11.

——. 1999. Para una teoría literaria hispanoamericana: A veinte años de un debate decisivo. *Revista de Crítica Literaria Latinoamericana* 50:9–12.

Coutinho, Edilberto. 1994. *Gilberto Freyre.* Rio de Janeiro: Agir.

dos Santos, Theotonio. 1970. The Structure of Dependence. *The American Economic Review* 60(2):231–36.

Driscoll, Barbara A. 1993. *'La Frontera' and Its People: The Early Development of Border and American Studies.* East Lansing, Mich.: Julián Samora Research Institute, Michigan State University.

Fernández, Enrique. 1988. Liner notes. Los Van Van. *Songo.* Mango Records compact disc 9825.

Flores Galindo, Alberto. 1980. *La agonía de Mariátegui.* Lima: Desco.

——. 1988. Uchuraccay: el psicoanálisis como metáfora. In *Tiempo de plagas,* 179–84. Lima: El Caballo Rojo.

Formell, Juan. 1998. La timba cubana en Uruguay con Los Van Van. Interview by Rosario Castellanos and Enrique Cotelo. Radio El Espectador, 27

October. Transcript retrieved 10 June 2001, from the World Wide Web: http://www.espectador.com/text/clt10272.htm.

Freyre, Gilberto. [1933] 1995. *Casa-Grande e Senzala: Formação da família Brasileira sob o regime da economia patriarcal*. Rio de Janeiro: Record.

———. 1940. *O mundo que o Português criou: aspecto das relações sociaes e do cultura do Brasil com Portugal e as colonias portuguesas*. Rio de Janeiro: José Olympio.

———. 1956. *The Masters and the Slaves: A Study in the Development of Brazilian Civilization*. 2d. English language edition. Translated by Samuel Putnam. New York: Knopf.

Furé, Rogelio Martínez. 1991. Regarding Folklore. In *Essays in Cuban Music: North American and Cuban Perspectives*. Edited by Peter Manuel, 251–65. Lanham, Md.: University Press of America.

Garcia, Manny, Jordan Levin, and Peter Whoriskey. 1999. The Sound and the Fury: Van Van's Music Brings Fans Together Despite City Division. *Miami Herald,* 10 October, p. 1A.

García Canclini, Néstor. 1995. *Hybrid Cultures: Strategies for Entering and Leaving Modernity*. Translated by Christopher L. Chiappari and Silvia L. López. Minneapolis: University of Minnesota Press.

Gibson, Charles. 1966. *Spain in America*. New York: Viking.

González Prada, Manuel. 1976. *Páginas libres/horas de lucha*. Caracas: Biblioteca Ayacucho.

Grandis, Rita de. 1997. Incursiones en torno a hibridación, una propuesta para discussion: de la mediación lingüística de Bajtin a la mediación simbólica de García Canclini. *Revista de Crítica Literaria Latinoamericana* 46:37–51.

Guillén, Nicolás. 1952. La canción del bongó. In *Sónsoro cosongo, motivos de son, West Indies Ltd., España: poema en cuatro angustias y una esperanza*. Buenos Aires: Losada.

Haberly, David. 1983. *Three Sad Races: Racial Identity and National Consciousness in Brazilian Literature*. Cambridge: Cambridge University Press.

Helg, Aline. 1990. Race in Argentina and Cuba, 1880–1930: Theory, Policies, and Popular Reaction. In *The Idea of Race in Latin America, 1870–1940*. Edited by Richard Graham, 37–69. Austin: University of Texas Press.

Herder, Johann Gottfried von. 1969. Essay on the Origin of Language. In *J. G. Herder on Social and Political Culture,* translated and edited by F. M. Barnard, 117–77. Cambridge: Cambridge University Press.

Holanda, Sérgio Buarque de. [1936] 1995. *Raízes do Brasil*. São Paulo: Companhia das Letras.

Horsman, Reginald. 1981. *Race and Manifest Destiny: The Origins of American Racial Anglo-Saxonism*. Cambridge, Mass.: Harvard University Press.

Hostos, Eugenio María de. 1939. El cholo. In *Temas sudamericanos. Obras completas,* vol. 7, 152–55. Havana: Cultural, S.A.

Jameson, Fredric. 1998. Marxism and the Historicity of Theory: An Interview with Fredric Jameson. By Xudong Zang. *New Literary History* 29(3): 353–83.

Jara, René, and Nicholas Spadaccini. 1992. Introduction: The Construction of a Colonial Imaginary: Columbus's Signature. In *The Amerindian Images and the Legacy of Columbus.* Edited by René Jara and Nicholas Spadaccini, 1–95. Minneapolis: University of Minnesota Press.

Kahn, Joel S. 1995. *Culture, Multiculture, Postculture.* London: Sage.

Knight, Alan. 1990. Revolution and Indigenismo: Mexico, 1920–1940. In *The Idea of Race in Latin America, 1870–1940.* Edited by Richard Graham, 71–102. Austin: University of Texas Press.

Kristeva, Julia. 1991. *Strangers to Ourselves.* Translated by Leon S. Roudiez. New York: Columbia University Press.

Kutzinki, Vera M. 1993. *Sugar's Secrets: Race and the Erotics of Cuban Nationalism.* Charlottesville: University Press of Virginia.

Larsen, Neil. 1997. Poverties of Nations: *The Ends of the Earth,* "Monetary Subjects without Money," and Postcolonial Theory. *Cultural Logic* 1(1): 20 pars. Retrieved 8 June 2001 from the World Wide Web: http://eserver.org/clogic/1-1/larsen.html.

Lea, Henry Charles. 1901. *The Moriscos: Their Conversion and Expulsion.* Philadelphia: Lea Brothers.

Lemaire, Ria. 1989. Re-Reading *Iracema:* The Problem of Women in the Construction of a National Brazilian Identity. *Luso-Brazilian Review* 26:59–73.

Limón, José E. 1998. *American Encounters: Greater Mexico, the United States, and the Erotics of Culture.* Boston: Beacon Press.

Lira, Andrés, and Luis Muro. 1987. El siglo de la integración. In *Historia general de México.* Edited by Daniel Cosío Villegas, 371–467. Mexico City: El Colegio de México.

Losada, Alejandro. 1983. *La literatura en la sociedad de América Latina: Perú y el Río de la Plata 1837–1880.* Frankfurt: Vervuert.

Malinowski, Bronislaw. [1940] 1995. Introduction. In *Cuban Counterpoint: Tobacco and Sugar,* by Fernando Ortiz, lvii–lxiv. Durham, N.C.: Duke University Press.

Manuel, Peter. 1991. Musical Pluralism in Revolutionary Cuba. In *Essays in Cuban Music.* Edited by Peter Manuel, 285–311. Lanham, Md.: University Press of America.

Mariátegui, José Carlos. [1928] 1981. *Siete ensayos de interpretación de la realidad peruana.* Lima: Amauta.

———. 1971. *Seven Interpretive Essays on Peruvian Reality.* Translated by Marjory Urquidi. Austin: University of Texas Press.

———. 1980. *Ideología y política.* Lima: Amauta.

——. 1981a. El destino de Norteamérica. In *Defensa del Marxismo*, 145–50. Lima: Amauta.

——. 1981b. *Peruanicemos al Perú*. Lima: Amauta.

——. 1996. *The Heroic and Creative Meaning of Socialism: Selected Essays of José Carlos Mariátegui*. Edited and Translated by Michael Pearlman. Atlantic Highlands, N.J.: Humanities Press.

Mariátegui, José Carlos, and Hugo Pesce. 1980. El problema de las razas en América Latina. In Mariátegui, *Ideología y política*, 21–86.

——. 1996. The indigenous question. In *The Heroic and Creative Meaning of Socialism: Selected Essays of José Carlos Mariátegui*. Edited and Translated by Michael Pearlman, 94–109. Atlantic Highlands, N.J.: Humanities Press.

Martius, Karl Friedrich Phillipp von. 1967. How the History of Brazil Should Be Written. Translated by Norris Lyle. In *Perspectives on Brazilian History*. Edited by E. Bradford Burns, 21–41. New York: Columbia University Press.

Marx, Karl, and Friedrich Engels. 1964. *The Communist Manifesto*. Translated by Samuel Moore. New York: Washington Square Press.

Mauleon, Rebecca, and Rachel Faro. 1999. Liner Notes. Los Van Van. *The Legendary Los Van Van: 30 Years of Cuba's Greatest Dance Band*. Ashé compact discs 2007a and 2007b.

Medeiros, Maria Alice de Aguiar. 1984. *O elogio da dominação: relendo 'Casa-Grande e Senzala.'* Rio de Janeiro: Achiamé.

Michaelsen, Scott. 1998. Hybrid Bound. Review of *Border Matters: Remapping American Cultural Studies. Postmodern Culture* 3 (May): 18 pars. Retrieved 6 June 1999, from the World Wide Web: http://muse.jhu.edu/journals /postmodern_culture/voo8/8.3r_michaelsen.html.

Moliner, María. [1966] 1990. *Diccionario de uso del español*. Madrid: Greidos.

Moore, Robin. 1997. *Nationalizing Blackness: Afrocubanismo and Artistic Revolution in Havana, 1920–1940*. Pittsburgh, Pa.: University of Pittsburgh Press.

Mota, Carlos Guilherme. 1980. *Ideologia da cultura brasileira (1933–1974): pontos de partida para uma revisão histórica*. São Paulo: Editora Ática.

Nascimento, Abdias do, and Elisa Larkin Nascimento. 1992. *Africans in Brazil: A Pan-African Perspective*. Trenton, N.J.: Africa World Press.

Nericcio, William. 1994. Review of *Days of Obligation: An Argument with My Mexican Father*, by Richard Rodriguez. *World Literature Today* 68 (Winter):141.

Nicholls, William. 1993. *Christian Anti-Semitism: A History of Hate*. Northvale, N.J.: Jason Aronson.

Olmedo, José Joaquín de. 1979. La victoria de Junín: canto a Bolívar. In *Poesía de la independencia*. Edited by Emilio Carilla, 8–33. Caracas: Biblioteca Ayacucho.

Ortiz, Fernando. [1940] 1995. *Cuban Counterpoint: Tobacco and Sugar.* Translated by Harriet de Onís. Durham, N.C.: Duke University Press.

Oviedo, José Miguel. 1965. *Genio y figura de Ricardo Palma.* Buenos Aires: Editorial Universitaria de Buenos Aires.

Palma, Ricardo. 1953. *Tradiciones peruanas completas.* Madrid: Aguilar.

Paz, Octavio. 1985. The Labyrinth of Solitude. In *The Labyrinth of Solitude, the Other Mexico, and Other Essays.* Translated by Lysander Kemp, Yara Milos, and Rachel Phillips Belash. New York: Grove Press.

——. 1988. *Sor Juana or the Traps of Faith.* Translated by Margaret Sayers Peden. Cambridge, Mass.: Harvard University Press.

Perera, Victor. 1993. Labyrinth of Solitude. Review of *Days of Obligation: An Argument with My Mexican Father. The Nation,* 18 January pp. 63–65.

Pérez Firmat, Gustavo. 1996. Richard Rodriguez and the Art of Abstraction. *Colby Quarterly* 32 (December):255–66.

Pérez-Torres, Rafael. 1997. Refiguring Aztlán. *Aztlán* 22(2):15–41.

Quijano, Aníbal. 1995. Modernity, Identity, and Utopia in Latin America. Translated by Michael Aronna. In *The Postmodernism Debate in Latin America.* Edited by John Beverley, José Oviedo, and Michael Aronna, 201–16. Durham, N.C.: Duke University Press.

Rama, Ángel. 1982. *Transculturación narrativa en América Latina.* México: Siglo XXI.

Rangel, Maria Lucia. 1997. Classico de Gilberto Freyre en fin sai do papel. *O Estado de São Paulo,* 1 November. Internet Edition. Retrieved 9 June 2001 from the World Wide Web. http://www.estado.com.br/edicao/pano/97/10/31/ca2531.html

Ribeiro, Darcy. 1986. Gilberto Freyre: uma introdução a *Casa-Grande e senzala.* In *Sobre o óbvio,* 109–73. Rio de Janeiro: Guanabara.

Riva Agüero, José de la. 1955. *Paisajes peruanos.* Lima: Imprenta Santa María.

——. 1962. La gran velada en honor de D. Ricardo Palma. In *Estudios de literatura peruana: del Inca Garcilaso a Eguren,* 357–60. Lima: Pontificia Universidad Católica.

Rodriguez, Richard. 1982. *Hunger of Memory: The Education of Richard Rodriguez.* Boston: David R. Godine.

——. 1992. *Days of Obligation: An Argument with My Mexican Father.* New York: Viking.

——. 1993. Author Savors the Melting Pot as the Perfect Brew. Interview with Richard Rodriguez. By Christopher Caldwell. *Insight on the News,* 4 January, p. 14–17.

——. 1995a. The Strong Man Is Unmasked as Everyman. *Los Angeles Times,* 19 February, Opinion section, p. 1.

——. 1995b. Prophets without Papers. *Harper's,* 23 April, p. 21.

——. 1995c. An Ancient Catholic. Interview with Richard Rodriguez. By Paul Crowley. *America,* 23 September, pp. 8–11.

——. 1995d. The New Native Americans. *Los Angeles Times,* 10 September, Opinion section, p. 1.

——. 1998a. The Browning of America. "The NewsHour with Jim Lehrer." Public Broadcasting System, 18 February. Transcript retrieved 28 May 2001, from the World Wide Web: http://www.pbs.org/newshour/essays /febru ary98/Rodriguez_2-18.html.

——. 1998b. A Campaign for Another Country. *Los Angeles Times,* 31 May, Opinion section, p. 1.

——. 1998c. Speaking American. "The NewsHour with Jim Lehrer." Public Broadcasting System, 9 June. Transcript retrieved 28 May 2001, from the World Wide Web: http://www.pbs.org/newshour/essays /june98/speaking _6-2.html.

——. 1998d. Language or Silence. "The NewsHour with Jim Lehrer." Public Broadcasting System, 15 September. Transcript retrieved 28 May 2001, from the World Wide Web: http://www.pbs.org/newshour/essays/rodri guez_9-15.html.

Rodriguez, Silvio. 1991. *Cuando digo futuro.* Fonomusic compact disc 1095.

Rodríguez-Arenas, Flor Maria. 1993. Historia editorial y literaria. In Ricardo Palma. *Tradiciones peruanas.* Edited by Julio Ortega, 341–408. Madrid: Archivos.

Saintoul, Catherine. 1988. *Racismo, etnocentrismo y literatura.* Translated by Catherine Saintoul and María del Carmen Guerra. Buenos Aires: Ediciones del Sol.

Saldívar, José David. 1997. *Border Matters: Remapping American Cultural Studies.* Berkeley: University of California Press.

Schutte, Ofelia. 1993. *Cultural Identity and Social Liberation in Latin American Thought.* Albany: State University of New York Press.

Schwamborn, Ingrid. 1990. *A recepção dos romances indianistas de José de Alencar.* Fortaleza-Ceará: UFC–Casa de José de Alencar.

Skidmore, Thomas. 1974. *Black into White: Race and Nationality in Brazilian Thought.* New York: Oxford University Press.

Sommer, Doris. 1991. *Foundational Fictions: The National Romances of Latin America.* Berkeley: University of California Press.

Sorel, Georges. 1972. *Reflections on Violence.* Translated by T. E. Hulme. New York: Collier.

Stalin, Joseph V. 1975. Marxism and the National Question. In *Marxism and the National-Colonial Question: A Collection of Articles and Speeches,* 15–99. San Francisco: Proletarian Publishers.

Stam, Robert. 1997. *Tropical Multiculturalism: A Comparative History of Race in Brazilian Cinema and Culture*. Durham, N.C.: Duke University Press.

Stavans, Ilan. 1993. The Journey of Richard Rodriguez. Review of *Days of Obligation: An Argument with My Mexican Father* by Richard Rodriguez/*Hunger of Memory* by Richard Rodriguez. *Commonweal,* 26 March, pp. 20–24.

Stewart, Charles. 1999. Syncretism and Its Synonyms: Reflections on Cultural Mixture. *Diacritics* 29(3):40–62.

Unzueta, Fernando. 1993. Las *Tradiciones* y la cuestión nacional. In *Tradiciones peruanas*. Edited by Julio Ortega, 503–19. Madrid: Archivos.

Valente, Luis Fernando. 1994. Palmilhando a tradição alencariana: um modelo intertextual de história literaria. *Revista de Crítica Literaria Latinoamericana* 40:141–54.

Los Van Van. 1989. *The Legendary Los Van Van/Thirty Years of Cuba's Greatest Dance Band*. Ashé Records compact disc 2007a/b.

———. 1999. *Llegó Van Van/Van Van Is Here*. Atlantic Records/Havana Caliente compact disc 83227-2.

Vasconcelos, José. 1997. *The Cosmic Race: A Bilingual Edition*. Translated by Didier T. Jaén. Baltimore, Md.: John Hopkins University Press.

Villaça, Alcides. 2000. Afterword: Iracema, Poetry, and Colonization. In *Iracema: A Novel by José de Alencar*. Translated by Clifford E. Landers, 139–48. New York: Oxford University Press.

Wasserman, Renata. 1994. *Exotic Nations: Literature and Cultural Identity in the United States and Brazil, 1830–1930*. Ithaca, N.Y.: Cornell University Press.

Williams, Raymond. 1983. *Keywords: A Vocabulary of Culture and Society*. Rev. ed. New York: Oxford University Press.

Young, Robert J. C. 1995. *Colonial Desire: Hybridity in Theory, Culture, and Race*. New York: Routledge.

Zilberman, Regina. 1977. *Do mito ao romance: tipologia da ficção brasileira contemporánea*. Porto Alegre: Universidade de Caxias do Sul.

index

mestizaje (*continued*)
18–19; and nation, 18–19, 30, 41; and race, 18–19. *See also* discourse of mestizaje; melting pot; mestizo; miscegenation

mestizo, 18, 108, 110, 117, 123, 132n. 12. *See also* mestizaje

Mexican Americans, 105–6. *See also* Chicanos/as

Mexico, 22–23, 106–8, 111–13, 140n. 13

Michaelsen, Scott, 142–43n. 3

migration, 9, 15, 17–18, 113, 121, 122, 124–26

Milanés, Pablo, 142n. 8

Milhaud, Darius, 79

miscegenation: in Brazil, 57–58, 60–63; in Cuba, 95–96, 99; contrasted with mestizaje, xiii, 18–19; in Mexico, 106–7; in Peru, 88–89, 91; and racialism, 3, 15–16; social effects of, 58–59, 61, 106, 115–16; in the United States, 4, 108–9; and whitening, 17–18, 60–61. *See also* cosmic race; mestizaje; racialism; whitening

modernity, 74, 89–92, 125

Moore, Robin D., 96, 97

More, Federico, 139n. 6

Moreno, Martim, 45. See also *Iracema*

mulata, 67, 96

multiculturalism, 25, 101, 117, 123

nation: and culture, 20–22, 29–30; and language, 13–14, 24, 33–37, 70–71, 103–5; and multiculturalism, 25, 122–24; and race, 11–15, 19–21, 29; role of Amerindians in definition of, 24, 30–32, 40–41, 53–54, 55–56, 82; role of blacks in definition of, 57, 71–72, 94–99; and socialism,

82–84, 91–92. *See also* discourse of mestizaje; identity; melting pot; mestizaje; multiculturalism

negrito, 96–99

neoculturation, 5

Nericcio, William, 142–43n. 3

new mestiza, 115–16, 120

Nietzsche, Friedrich, 73, 139n. 3

Olmedo, José Joaquín de, 23

Ortiz, Fernando, 5–7, 9–10

Palma, Ricardo, xiv, 23, 27–41, 43, 44, 53, 75, 136n. 12, 139n. 6

Paz, Octavio, 22–23, 107, 140n. 13, 143n. 5, 144n. 9

Pedro I (Emperor of Brazil), 53

Pedro II (Emperor of Brazil), 43

Pérez Firmat, Gustavo, 143n. 4, 144n. 13

Pérez-Torres, Rafael, 145n. 19

Peru, 27–30, 31–32, 74–75, 77–79, 83–84, 88, 89–90, 120–21, 123–26

Pesce, Hugo, 78, 86

Picasso, Pablo, 79

postcolonialism, 126

Poti, 45, 48. See also *Iracema*

Quechua, 29, 33–34, 36, 44, 77–78, 79, 84, 88, 89–91. *See also* Amerindian

Quijano, Aníbal, 73

race, 11–25, 59–60, 86–87, 105–6, 131n. 1. *See also* culture; discourse of mestizaje; mestizaje; miscegenation; racialism

racial democracy, xv, 61, 70

racialism: criticism of, 19, 87–88, 131n. 6, 133n. 14; Freyre and, 55, 57, 59–61, 62–63, 65; and Latin America, 3, 14–19; Mariátegui and, 86–89;

about the author

Born in Lima, Peru, Juan Enrique De Castro received his undergraduate degree in English from California State University, Los Angeles (1992), and his M.A. and doctorate in comparative literature from the University of Southern California (1998). He has written several articles on constructions of race and nation and on the literary criticism of José Carlos Mariátegui. He has taught courses in Spanish language and Spanish and Spanish American literature at the University of Southern California and at the California Institute of Technology (1996–2001). Currently, he is on the faculty of the Division of Liberal Arts and International Studies at the Colorado School of Mines, where he is an assistant professor of comparative literature.